THE NATURE OF CULTURAL THINGS

STUDIES IN
Anthropology

Consulting Editors:

MORTON H. FRIED
AND MARVIN HARRIS
Columbia University

THE NATURE OF CULTURAL THINGS

Marvin Harris
Columbia University

RANDOM HOUSE
NEW YORK

FIRST PRINTING

Library of Congress Catalog Card Number: 63-19713

MANUFACTURED IN THE UNITED STATES OF AMERICA BY
THE BOOK PRESS, BRATTLEBORO, VERMONT

Design by Margaret F. Plympton

Introduction

I have attempted here to show how a taxonomy of cultural things can be grounded in the observation of the nonverbal behavior of individuals. The result is, properly speaking, a "meta-taxonomy," since its constituent categories are found not among particular actors, but in all large human populations.* These categories are defined by explicit sets of observational procedures or "operations," all of which ultimately refer back to the behavior of individuals, and relate to each other as elements in a hierarchy of logical and empirical constructs.

In building this hierarchy, I have tried to separate the explanation of cultural things from their definition. The definition of phenomena, it seems to me, ought not to depend upon assumptions and theories that a study of those phenomena intends to verify. For that reason I do not start out with declarations that culture is exclusively learned behavior, that culture is unique to human beings,

* In the terminology of George Gaylord Simpson (1961:19), the cultural things with which we shall be concerned are "categories" rather than "Taxa." That is, they logically correspond not to entities like Chordates, Mammals, and Primates, but to Phylum, Class, and Order.

that culture is a homeostatic system, that culture is dependent upon the use of symbols, that culture is passed on from one generation to the next, or that culture is the product of human interaction. Alfred Kroeber's remark that how culture "comes to be is really more distinctive of culture than what it is" (1948:253), strikes me as putting the cart before the horse. How culture comes to be, what it does or doesn't do, are questions that cannot be settled by definitions. Indeed, these questions are meaningless unless we agree on the range of phenomena to which they will be applied.

Because I have made—or believe I have made—very few *a priori* assumptions about the causal, dynamic, or structural properties of culture, I have found it necessary to discard the nomenclature by which metataxonomic categories of cultural things are presently identified. I regret this necessity, but I can see no alternative. True enough, every social scientist already has a large collection of assorted bottles neatly labeled, "traits," "customs," "institutions," "roles," and the like. But these bottles are so stuffed with words—words taken from the dictionary, words referring to other words—that there is no room to pour anything new into them. To advance beyond the present state of Platonic essences and tautologies, culture and cultural things must be defined in terms of the instruments, calibrations, processes, and activities—the *operations* by which observers can get to know about them. I wish to assure the reader that I do *not* delight in being obscure. I have invented new terms because I have had to identify "things" which do not correspond to any "things" which our orthodox terminology has the power to specify.

Aside from the difficulty of this necessary, but burdensome, plethora of new terms, the ensuing discussion suffers from a rather striking paradox. As I have indicated, this book attempts to develop a meta-taxonomy of cultural parts which will be simultaneously logical, empirical, and hierarchical. By "hierarchical" I mean that all the higher-order entities are to be constructed out of the lower-order ones. Starting with the simplest behavior unit, I have tried to show how independent observers can expect to identify intersubjectively valid cultural entities of the most abstract sort. But while I have attempted to offer examples of the kinds of empirical entities that exist on each of the levels of classification above the bedrock data of unique individual behavior, I have been able to provide only a step-by-step demonstration of the required operations for relatively low-order categories. Since it is my contention that the operations necessary for the construction of more abstract units are pragmatically feasible, the reader is free to adopt a "show-me" attitude. If it can be done, why haven't I done it? My defense is simply that I had neither the time, money, nor the staff for the vast amount of labor that would have been involved. This is regrettable, but I do not think it is fatal to the approach. That it is impossible to place a man on Mars because Congress will not appropriate the necessary budget, is unsound reasoning. If scientists know what steps must be taken, and if these steps violate no fundamental principles of mechanics, then a trip to Mars is indeed possible. Just so, my argument for the possibility of an operationalized account of complex institutions: I haven't done it, but I can marshal convincing evidence to show that it is manpower rather than technique which is lacking.

The same flaw in even more glaring form is to be found in the claims I have made for the intersubjective identification of both lower- and higher-order cultural categories. In neither case can I report that independent observers have followed the operations and achieved substantially similar results. I simply argue that with a reasonable amount of training any number of independent observers can learn to employ the operations by which the empirical instances of the meta-taxonomic categories are to be identified. I believe, in short, that given sufficient resources, we could develop intersubjective and culture-free descriptions of cultural things. Again, the reader is entitled to say "show-me." And again my defense is that the resources necessary for a large-scale demonstration through empirical trials were not available. It seems to me, however, that before such large-scale empirical trials can be attempted, it is important to have argued for the feasibility and potential advantage of the proposed method.

Having apologized for the book's most conspicuous shortcomings, it may not be out of place to emphasize some of its strong points. I may have given the impression that the attempt to create an operational data language is to be judged for its programmatic worth as a research proposal. This is certainly among my intentions, but is of minor significance in the present context. Regardless of whether or not the missing operations are ever performed, the meta-analysis upon which they must be based is of immediate import for orienting research and theory in cultural anthropology. To be sure, I have fallen far short of the standards I set for myself. But I do not believe that I have fallen as far as most of the attempts I have read by others to define culture and cultural things. I have, at least, actually carried out some of the indicated operations and have attempted to specify what additional operations ought to be performed. My definitions of cultural things are not purely operational, but I regard it as an advance to have at least explored what would be required to make them operationally viable in the strictest sense. Thus, my ultimate defense is that the meta-taxonomy of cultural parts is equivalent to a model by which current descriptive practices can be judged. There are degrees of approximation to this model. No one may ever fully achieve the ultimate measure of precision and intersubjectivity which it calls for, but we may nonetheless get considerably closer than has been the case up to now.

I should like to acknowledge the support of the Social Science Research Council whose grant made the writing of this book possible, and to thank Mrs. Nan Pendrell for her generously given editorial assistance.

CONTENTS

THE NATURE OF CULTURAL THINGS

I

The Nature of Things

Empirical Things

In setting out to identify cultural things, I shall be guided by the assumption that it is desirable to bestow upon them an epistemological status logically equivalent to the status of the entities which are the object of inquiry in the physical sciences. Such things enjoy what is generally called an empirical epistemological status. To say that this is desirable is not to commit oneself on the issue of whether or not it is possible. Just what degree of epistemological resemblance between cultural and physical things can in fact be achieved remains to be seen.

According to philosopher-physicist Percy W. Bridgman, a term may be said to acquire its particular epistemological status in accordance with the type of logical and behavioral procedures or operations by which it is related to its referent. Hence, to bestow an empirical status upon cultural things, it would seem that one need merely emulate the operations characteristic of the physical sciences. This view, however, presupposes that physical scientists agree upon the criteria which are necessary and sufficient for an empirical approach. Agreement does exist to the extent that the specification of operations is regarded as a prime responsibility of any practicing scientist. But which operations are to be permitted and which rejected constitutes a continuing polemic among philosophers and philosophically-minded scientists. Indeed, very different kinds of logical and empirical procedures have been invoked under the catch-all of "operation":

> Interpreting Bridgman more liberally, we can readily detect in his writings at least two meanings of the term "operation"—one specific or narrow, and the other general or broad. The specific use restricts the word to physical operations, and even at times to metrical operations. The general use allows mental, verbal and 'pencil and paper' operations to be included under the term. (Benjamin, 1955:4-5)

Disagreement as to what constitutes a valid empirical operation is characterized by an increasing penumbra of doubt as one moves from the narrow to the broad construal of operationism. Very subtle technical arguments must be employed if one is intent upon delimiting the total range of valid empirical operations. However, well-nigh perfect agreement reigns about what is empirical in the narrowest sense. Thus the amateur philosopher need not venture very far into this philosophical jungle. The narrow construal of empirical operationism is sufficiently clear to serve as a model against which the attempt to develop a data language appropriate to cultural things may be judged. Since the physical sciences do not restrict their operations to this narrow range of procedures, it is scarcely to be expected that cultural anthropology will do so. But there is no reason to suppose that the grounds and direction of departure will be the same for each science. It is the obligation of the philosopher to construct a model of empirical operations broad enough to encompass the practices of all of the sciences. It is the obligation of the cultural anthropologist to show why, in his particular case, the narrowest construal of empirical operations is inadequate for a successful science of culture. If the reasons for departing from the strict physicalist model of operationism are spelled out with sufficient clarity, the larger task of deciding whether or not the practices at issue conform to general empiricist doctrine may be left with equanimity to the philosophers and logicians.

Operational Purity

According to the narrowest operational point of view, a thing is defined by the interaction of an observer and a measuring device at a specified spatio-temporal locus. The observer tries to restrict his utterances to accounts of the following sort: "I am speaking of that entity *X* which was of dimension *N* on apparatus *P* when I applied *P* to *S* sector of *F* field of inquiry with movements *a, b, c . . .* of my body." Things identified in this fashion clearly conform to the notion of empirical epistemological status. But even at this bedrock level of empirical discourse, a number of unoperationalized terms must be accepted in order to avoid an infinite and fruitless regress in search of absolute operational purity. Thus, the meaning of "observer" and aspects of the characterization of the measuring device must be taken for granted. Similarly, the specification of the spatio-temporal locus must start from a field of inquiry, some aspects of which possess the status of primitive givens, while the description of the manipulative behavior must also rest upon many undefined words having to do with complex motions of the parts of the human body.

That complete operational purity is an unobtainable goal does not necessarily diminish the value of the empiricist position, although it does render the survival of alternative epistemological approaches more intelligible. If we gratuitously assume the existence of certain entities in order to operationalize others, why not assume the existence of any entities whatsoever? This question will not be pursued here for obvious reasons. But it is worth keeping in mind as a guard against overly glib formulations of the empiricist program. Let it suffice to say that empiricism is distinguished by its readiness to pare down its unoperationalized givens to a minimum, whenever it is challenged to do so.

Dependence upon primitive terms is by no means the weakest aspect of operationalism, conceived in its narrowest sense. When the operational point of view is pressed to its limit of terminological precision and clarity, it fails utterly to provide a practical basis for scientific communication. Bridgman's early dictum, "The concept is synonymous with the corresponding set of operations" (1927:5), cannot, if literally interpreted, serve as the working model for anything resembling normal scientific activity, even in the physical sciences. A data language constructed out of terms introduced in the above fashion would guarantee intersubjective objectivity, but virtually eliminate intersubjective communication. Every word in the data language would stand for a nicely defined operation, but every operation would call for a different word. Communication would, in effect, consist of an ever-expanding array of proper nouns about which it would be impossible to make relational or connective statements.

Strict operationism, in company with any thoroughgoing brand of empiricism, must at the outset come to grips with the unavoidable fact that if empirical things are to be the subject of scientific discourse, they must be treated as constructs or abstractions. This is so because no two operations and hence no two things can ever be shown through empirical operations alone to be precisely identical; whereas it can almost always be shown that any two entities are definitely not precisely identical. A science which deals only with unique entities cannot even begin to do its job since its discourse will consist merely of endless cataloguing of unique things.

Identical Things

The nonidentity of all things is guaranteed by the fact that all observational procedures involve some kind of measuring operation. Every measuring operation in turn involves some implicit or explicit scale or calibration. Each time a measuring operation is performed it is possible to perform it again with a more precise calibration and arrive at a different specification of the thing under consideration. It is empirically known that the regress in search of precision must ultimately terminate in calibrations which are as fine as microparticles and about whose position and velocity there is the built-in indeterminacy of Heisenberg's principle. Bridgman himself was fully aware of this dilemma: "It is a general consequence of the approximate character of all measurement that no empirical science can ever make exact statements" (1927:34).

The ultimate indeterminacy of measurements means that it can never be demonstrated that two macro-entities are exactly alike. On the other hand, it is known empirically that all entities, with the possible exception of microparticles (Hanson, 1958), can definitely be shown to be different from all other entities, including themselves. When very precise calibrations are employed, this positive difference can be demonstrated without resorting to finer calibrations. Some of these differences are apparent to the human observer even when extremely crude measuring operations are employed. Thus, an ordinary ruler shows that a living plant changes from day to day. Many things, when measured against the background of relatively slowly changing entities, appear to the unaided human eye to be changing very rapidly. Smoke rising, trees swaying, cars moving, and people walking change from moment to moment in ways that are strikingly apparent to the human senses. Other things, however, appear to be stable and at rest from moment to moment. But when finer calibrations are made, they too can be shown to be undergoing changes, as signaled by slight differences in the alignment of sensitive measuring instruments.

Suppose we wish to define a penny. First, the space-time locus of the penny is subjected to a series of measuring operations by which its physical and chemical properties and its dimensions and position can be specified. We have now identified a thing. But as Heraclitus long ago noted, if we repeat our defining operations on the next day, we shall find the penny is no longer the same thing. No matter how rapidly we repeat our observations, or how often, we will always come up with a somewhat different set of defining characters. How then can one talk about a penny as if it were a single thing, when in fact it can be shown to be a plurality of things, whose number is limited only by the refinement of our observational operations and the time at our disposal?

Classes of Things

The way out of this dilemma is provided by the logical operation known as *classification*. Although it is empirically impossible to discover identities in nature, it is possible to create the logico-empirical relationship of similarity. If every pointer reading differs from every other, then the differences between the readings are themselves not identical. Sometimes the whole sweep of an instrument's dial is at stake; in other cases, only microscopic deflections occur. Continuing with the narrow operational point of view, we may say that to classify is to group pointer readings or other instrumentally obtained measurements into relatively small or relatively large differences.

Although the process of classification is popularly described as finding the "same" property in a collection of different entities, this is patently not the case. Sameness is a purely logical relationship which can be demonstrated for logical constructs, but not for empirical entities. Whenever sameness is applied in the context of operationally valid macro-entities, it only means that, according to some metrical standard, two readings on a measuring device do not differ by more than a specified amount. For example, suppose we wish to establish a class of things which will include all entities similar to a particular penny. One property of the penny is that its diameter is more than $^{11}/_{16}$ but less than $^{12}/_{16}$ of an inch. Objects whose diameters fall clearly within these extremes share a property in common with the penny and are therefore similar to it, according to the particular criterion we have selected. Some objects will have diameters which fall so close to the extremes that we shall not be able to determine with certainty whether they belong in the same class. But there will be many objects about which we can be quite certain since no further refinement of measurement will push them outside of the delimited range. Any number of additional properties may now be added to the class criteria, provided that in each case we specify some range of variation. The penny varies from moment to moment, but as long as it falls within the stipulated range of variation, it continues to belong to the same class of things. The same is true of all the other class members.

This way of regarding a penny is strongly opposed to the ingrained instructions of common sense and ordinary language. English permits us to discourse quite freely about the "same" penny, book, person, institution, or culture. But an unbiased view of the things around us requires us to reject such claims. We can never speak about or point to the same empirical thing. *The "same" penny can never be anything more than a member of the same logical class of things to which the penny of a moment ago belonged.*

Despite the empirically inoperational status of the concept of identity, the literature of biology, psychology, sociology, and anthropology is replete with references to such mythical entities as identical genes, identical responses, and identical institutions. We are also constantly being told that some organisms, responses, or institutions are changing, while others remain fixed, static, or stable. It is time that these unfounded assertions were cast out of respectable scientific discourse. They contribute nothing but deliberate or incident obfuscation.

> Our use of static words is analogous to our analysis of the world around us into things—individual, discrete, constant, and static—whereas it has been obvi-

> ous from at least the time of the Greeks that 'all things flow.' (Bridgman, 1959:35)

Classification and Common Sense

Common sense is completely unreliable in the matter of classification. The common senses are automatic built-in classifiers which divide the world in a particular way without telling us how or why they are doing it. The common sense of sight leads us to talk about many objects as if they were the same from moment to moment. An uncommon sense of sight—an eye, for example, with the resolving power of an electron microscope—would make a mockery of our cherished stable common-sense objects.

> Solid matter, this most obtrusive part of experience and most trivial of the categories of naive physics, consists almost completely of holes, being a void for the greatest part, only interwoven by centers of energy which, considering their magnitude, are separated by astronomical distances. (Bertalanffy, 1955:247)

Creatures with senses fine enough to detect the world of microparticles might spend an eternity without discovering the properties common to that sector of universe which we gratuitously accept as an ordinary chair. The first of their kind to propose that the world contained stable macro-objects would no doubt be banished into the Siberia of anti-matter.

It is no accident that our senses automatically divide the world into apparently stable units which can serve as the descriptive entities in some (but not all) scientific laws. Our inborn cleverness with respect to certain types of classifications is the product of some two billion years of biological evolution.[1] Had our

[1] "The categories of experience have arisen in biological evolution and have continually to justify themselves in the struggle for existence" (Bertalanffy, 1955:256).

senses not acquired the ability to divide the world into those classes of macro-objects by means of which the laws of mechanics are formulated, we should not have evolved into what we are. Natural selection discovered the laws of classical physics long before Newton was born. These discoveries were made because it is often extremely useful for behaving organisms to respond *as if* two things are identical, even though they are empirically different. Human beings, like all macro-organisms, are dependent upon the perception of macro-objects for survival and reproduction. All animals must be able to push and pull, bite or swallow other macro-objects without having to take time out to specify which classificatory criteria they are using. They must automatically be able to perceive coherent patterns in the environment through successive time intervals despite the interminable changes taking place. The ability to classify, or as it is known in psychology, the ability to "generalize," is thus an endowment common to all grades of animal life.

One noxious consequence of common-sense classifications is that we tend to regard the macrolevel of familiar stable objects and their movements as comprising a realm of superior reality. Thus, we are constantly being told that common-sense things are "real," while the things created out of the logical and empirical labors of science are "merely" concepts, abstractions, models, heuristic devices, reifications, or hypothesized entities. The distinction implied by these terms ought, if anything, to be reversed. The empirical things for which a superior reality is normally reserved are usually the classes of empirical events most poorly defined by logical-empirical criteria; whereas the abstractions, concepts, and the like at least betray some awareness that a system of classification ought to be furnished. The chair you are sitting on is every bit as much an abstraction as an electron or totemism. The only difference is that practically no conscious effort has been made to formalize the classificatory procedure by which chairs are distinguished from people, but not distinguished from "themselves" during successive time intervals.

Natural Units

Many scientific workers suffer from the delusion that some unit things are more "natural" than others. Thus, atoms, species, genes, individual organisms, culture traits are frequently described as "natural units"—again, with the implication that they enjoy some sort of superior reality. Implicit in this notion is the belief that some entities are spatio-temporally continuous with themselves, but discontinuous with everything else. It should be clear, however, from what has been said about measurement, that nothing can be shown to be perfectly continuous with itself. The choice of units, therefore, must depend upon selecting certain kinds of discontinuities rather than others.

The natural units of science, and of ordinary discourse, are essentially customary devices which cannot be justified on purely logical grounds. Take the chair you are sitting on. Why do we consider it a unit? The chair has legs which sit upon the floor. You sit upon the chair. Why isn't "floor-chair-you" a thing, rather than the chair? You might argue that the chair is a separate entity because it can be separated from the floor and moved about as a unit. But the ability to be dismantled cannot relegate an entity to the status of not being a "natural" thing, since the chair, or any other entity (with the exception perhaps of some microparticles), can also be pulled, sawed, chopped, or blasted into smaller pieces. The truth is, all things are parts of parts of parts. Yet in everyday discourse, as well as in science, we dismantle a particular field of inquiry into certain units but not into others. Thus, the chair is regarded as a unit thing, whereas "floor-chair-you" sounds as if it belongs in a poem about purple cows. Neither unit, however, is more "natural" than the other.

Selection of Classificatory Criteria

If there are no natural units, what justification is there for dividing the world into certain unit-classes rather than others? Since empirical entities are defined by a particular set of operations, the number of entities that may be abstracted from any sector of the universe is limited only by the number and kinds of operations employed. Logic alone is of no assistance here. It tells us how to find similarities, but not which operations to select, nor what range of variation to specify.

Why a science elects to emphasize certain operations and metric differences rather than others can be understood only in relationship to the ultimate aims of scientific activity. If we wish to establish a class of data-language entities consisting of chair-man-floor, we may feel logically free to do so. But if one is performing these operations in the role of a scientist, he must be prepared to defend them in relation to certain scientific values *which are not an intrinsic part of narrow operationalism.*

The ultimate objective of scientific activity is the formulation of the lawful principles which govern the behavior of empirical things. Scientific laws are essentially brief statements about the behavior of things under stipulated conditions. The hallmark of a scientific law is that from it the behavior of a very large number of things can be predicted or retrodicted with a high degree of accuracy, despite the brevity of the initial statement. Prediction or retrodiction is made possible by the empirically established fact that certain classes of things behave in regular or repetitive ways under certain classes of conditions.

> The function of a science . . . is to establish general laws covering the behavior of empirical events or objects with which the science in question is concerned, and thereby to enable us to connect together

> our knowledge of the separately known events, and to make reliable predictions of events as yet unknown. (Braithwaite, 1953:1)

Because science is a goal-oriented activity, it is possible to judge scientific procedures from a value position. Thus, certain data-gathering or data-manipulating activities are said to be more scientific than others according to the degree with which they contribute to the formulation of scientific laws. In the game of science, one is obliged to consider all his moves in relation to this fundamental rule. Hence, the only exit from the dilemma of the discontinuity and nonidentity of all things is to inquire whether or not a particular mode of elementary classification is productive of scientific laws.

Obviously, not all conceivable classes of empirical things lend themselves equally to prediction and retrodiction. A data language could be developed which would never permit the formulation of lawful statements. For out of the theoretical infinity of classificatory modes, only a very few lead to prediction or retrodiction. In other words, it is always possible to classify things in ways which will make retrodiction or prediction unlikely. Had Galileo elected to make no distinction between animate and inanimate entities, he probably would never have been able to formulate the laws of inanimate macro-mechanics. Inanimate macro-entities tend to stay at rest until an outside force puts them into motion; organisms stop and go in very erratic ways. For Newton to formulate the principle of gravity, it was necessary to use a data language having terms for mass and acceleration. If he had included color or smell in the basic units, little merit would have been attached to his work.

The development of a data language is thus a completely pragmatic affair. A particular mode of classification is good or bad depending upon the kinds of results which can be achieved with it. If the classification reveals orderly relations, it is a good classification;

if it reveals nothing but chaos, it is worthless. As noted by George G. Simpson:

> Some classifications pertain to a wider range of inductions or to more meaningful generalizations than others and are in that sense "better" or more useful. (1961:25)

The psychologist B. F. Skinner has also defended the use of a data language (reinforcement theory) on the grounds that the descriptive results are orderly:

> The appearance of smooth curves in dynamic processes marks a unique point in the progressive restriction of a preparation, and it is to this uniquely determined entity that the term reflex may be assigned. A respondent . . . and operant are defined at levels of specification marked by the orderliness of dynamic changes. (Skinner, 1938:40)

When scientists refer to natural units, they are usually, if not invariably, referring to data-language units which have stood the test of the scientific ethic in that they have been fruitful of predictive or retrodictive statements. The epistemological status of such units, however, is beclouded by the additional circumstance that many data-language entities appear to correspond to the unoperationalized entities which are discriminated in ordinary discourse as a result of evolutionary processes having nothing whatsoever to do with scientific activity per se. Why this correspondence exists between some kinds of scientific things and the things of ordinary discourse has already been discussed. Ordinary language is the embodiment of countless untold experiments of both a biological and cultural nature during which the discrimination of certain classes of things has proved useful in the business of living. Not surprisingly some of these entities are also useful in the business of science.

That the units in a data language must ultimately be

judged for their contribution to lawful generalization seems incontrovertible. But how one is to decide which units are likely to be useful for the generation of lawful statements, prior to the formulation of such statements, remains an urgent practical problem. The choice of operations cannot be conducted on a purely trial and error basis, since the probability of blindly hitting upon a set of entities which exhibit regularities is greatly inferior to the probability of choosing entities which display no orderly relations with each other. This difficulty has been repeatedly exposed in criticisms of the Baconian notion of science as a purely inductive enterprise. Bacon proposed, in effect, that lawful generalizations would emerge automatically from the comparison of empirical facts collected at random. Critics of this view have conclusively shown that Bacon's expectation was hopelessly unrealistic. Not a single important theory in any of the sciences has been generated on a purely inductive basis. Unless the collection of facts is guided by some prior notion of what kinds of facts are likely to exhibit orderly relations, induction is doomed by the laws of chance to result in a monumental heap of scientifically valueless curiosities.[2]

To describe in detail how an expectation of orderly relationships informs the decision to concentrate on certain kinds of operations rather than others is beyond the compass of this book. The exact process probably varies from science to science and from individual to individual. In some cases, the operations are dictated by a fully evolved mathematico-deductive theory of how the field of inquiry is structured and how the elements in this structure behave in relationship to each other. Sometimes the decision is guided by common-sense notions of what the relevant entities ought to be like, without benefit of

[2] The antiscientific nature of pure induction is nowhere more apparent than in the work of Franz Boas and his students during the first half of this century (Cf. Beuttner-Janusch, 1957; Wax, 1956).

high-level theories. Or it involves various sorts of unconscious assumptions derived from common-sense categories or vague hunches based on dimly perceived analogies. All of these procedures are reputable, since, in the final analysis, what matters is not the deductive statements but their operationalized inductive counterparts or consequences. The only kind of deductive position which inspires suspicion is that which adamantly asserts that a particular choice of operations has been made without benefit of any assumptions whatsoever. In view of the determinate nature of most human behavior, it is highly unlikely that any scientific activity issues from a conceptual vacuum. Practical-minded people are very fond of simple, unadorned, plain, unembellished, and otherwise unencumbered "matters of fact," but no such animal exists. "When we make a so-called simple observation," Withers notes, "we only make it because there is some implicit conceptual framework into which it fits" (1959:94).

In this chapter it has not been my intention to set forth a complete and formalized version of an empirical theory of knowledge. Rather, I have been concerned with emphasizing certain salient epistemological issues which I deem essential for a theory of the knowledge of cultural things. Without a firm resolution of these issues sound progress cannot be achieved toward the formulation of culturological laws.

Thus far I have shown that the narrowest form of empiricism—the equation of the thing with an instrument-mediated measuring operation—must suffer certain compromises if it is to serve as a practical standard for any branch of the empirical sciences. First, the acceptance of undefined primitive entities, upon which the operations themselves are based, must precede the formulation of the data language. Second, data-language terms cannot have a pure empirical referent, but must refer instead to operations involving both logical and empirical procedures. And finally, the choice of logico-empirical operations must be guided by some prejudgment of what kinds of entities are likely to exhibit orderly relations.

As we shall see in the next chapter, empiricist doctrine must suffer additional compromises if it is to be useful in the identification of cultural things.

2

The Cultural Field of Inquiry

The identification of things whose epistemological status conforms to the highest canons of empiricism requires the conjunction of a field of inquiry, a measuring device, and logico-empirical measuring and classifying operations. Let us now consider to what extent and in what manner these requirements may be met in cultural anthropology.

The Cultural Field of Inquiry

The only criterion of a successful delimitation of a field of inquiry is whether or not a sufficiently large group of practicing scientists regard the field as worthy of their professional interest. It is useless to argue whether a particular construal of the cultural field of inquiry encompasses all the professional activities of all practicing cultural anthropologists. Since the delimitation of the field must take place through the medium of unoperationalized common-sense terms, all that is necessary is that the field be roughly approximate to the sector of the universe which is currently under study by a substantial percentage of cultural anthropologists. Genuine intellectual issues cannot exist with respect to what should or should not be included. Grounds for dispute are furnished only by proposals for dividing the field into operationally valid units. The field itself merely furnishes the raw materials upon which particular logico-empirical operations are brought to bear.

Without further apologies, I shall assert that human behavior constitutes the cultural field of inquiry. By human behavior, I mean the gross changes of state which the body parts of human beings exhibit. At the center of this field are the external body parts and the fairly rapid spatial displacements which they undergo from time to time. In common-sense parlance, a body part and its movements comprise an entity known as an action or an activity.

Internal Responses and Growth Responses

Both anthropologists and psychologists would agree that the movements of arms, legs, fingers, toes, mouths, sexual organs, and other external parts of the human body comprise responses well within a common field of inquiry. But it is not clear to what extent the internal organs of the body and their associated changes of state ought also to be regarded as part of the field. Psychologists usually leave the scientific identification of the internal body parts and their changes to physiologists. Yet, the movements of some internal parts, especially those connected with the body's orifices, such as the intestinal, urinogenital, and pulmonary tracts, are obviously portions of overlapping fields of interest shared by physiologists, psychologists, and anthropologists. The most important of these, from an anthropological viewpoint, are the organs of speech, the responses of which constitute an important concern of every ethnographic report. By way of analogy with the speech organs, I would suggest that the cultural field of inquiry includes those internal responses which are easily exposed to external observation by virtue of their direct effect upon external parts of the body or upon the body's immediate environment. The responses of organs deeply embedded within the body, whose effects are conveyed to the observer outside of the skin only through a complicated concatenation of intermediate response chains, will be regarded as entities peripheral to the main field.

Similar comments must be made with respect to those body changes which occur relatively slowly and are associated with maturation, growth, and senility. The growth of a limb or the development of dentition and secondary sexual traits might reasonably be regarded as bits of behavior, since they involve changes of state of body parts. There is no urgent need for including or excluding these responses in the cultural field of inquiry. They ought merely to be regarded as constituting a transition zone between the cultural field and the fields of other sciences.

Material Culture

One of the principal objections to the definition of the cultural field of inquiry in terms of human responses is that a considerable amount of ethnographic description is concerned with entities in the so-called "material culture." Insofar as we are concerned with the human responses of which material objects are the effects or products, this is no problem. The behavior responsible for the production of houses, tools, weapons, transportation devices, and the like, lies very much at the center of the field of inquiry. Yet, it is not clear how the objects themselves enter into the cultural field of inquiry without destroying the field's homogeneity.

Superficially, responses and material objects appear to belong to utterly different fields of inquiry. This is surely the case when a material object is subjected to the operations characteristic of the physical and chemical sciences. But when they are subject to other kinds of operations, they are very much a part of the cultural field. The reason for this, which will be made clear by the end of this chapter, is that the classification of human responses is unlikely to yield useful units *unless physical objects are employed as mediating or scene-setting criteria.*

Behavior Is Not Culture

For the moment, the only other point about the cultural field of inquiry requiring emphasis, is that the identification of the central portion of the field as human behavior does not in itself determine the nature of cultural things. The responses which comprise the cultural field of inquiry merely constitute a rough common-sense demarcation of that sector of the universe to which the observational procedures of cultural anthropology are to be primarily directed. *No assertion has been made that human responses are cultural things.* Indeed, to avoid misunderstanding on this historically touchy point, I should like to state that these common-sense entities *are definitely not* cultural things. Like any entities which form the subject of scientific discourse, they are admitted into scientific discourse only by virtue of the interaction of an observer, an operational procedure, and a field of inquiry. Thus far, I have merely described the field of inquiry and hence cannot on epistemological grounds have defined the nature of any scientifically valid entity. Certain operations applied to this field will result in the characterization of certain kinds of things; others will result in quite different kinds of things. If we subject this field to analysis by means of a geiger counter, we shall extract characterizations of microparticles. If we employ an electron microscope, we shall be on our way toward discovering the entities which science describes as genes and chromosomes. If we apply a sharp knife, we shall be able to create the world of things which form the subject of discourse in human anatomy and physiology. Other operational procedures, which remain to be specified, will result in the definition of the classes of cultural things.

Common Sense and the Behavior Stream

Human behavior is a great stream of uninterrupted events, consisting of the totality of the motions of the body parts of every human being who has ever lived. The continuity and contiguity of events in this prodigious behavior stream are part of the temporal and spatial continuum of the physical world. It is a scientific task of the highest priority to break this behavior stream into bits whose recurrences will provide the basis for lawful predictions. But in this realm, as in most sectors of the macrophysical world, the systematic classifications and predictions characteristic of the modern scientific enterprise have been preceded by at least 25,000 years of common-sense decisions. Every normal, semantically intact adult shares in an immense, informal, and unoperationalized scheme for breaking the behavior stream into recurrent units. Our ability to live and flourish is totally dependent upon the dexterity and accuracy with which we are able to isolate and predict "discrete" events in our own and related behavior streams. This facility is one of the grand achievements of the evolution of natural language.

Every natural language contains a set of terms and rules for combining events which are pragmatically appropriate for isolating and predicting important occurrences in the human behavior stream. And every normal human adult has learned how to apply these terms with sufficient facility to accomplish the most complex sorts of interaction with his human and nonhuman environment. The pragmatic worth of the vernacular divisions of the behavior stream is confirmed over and over during the course of an average day—when we make a purchase in a store, when we arrive at the appropriate time and place for a lecture, a show, a cocktail party. Whenever we act on the basis of information about where people will be and what they will be doing, and find our actions to be appropriate, we confirm the validity of the common-sense behavioral units.

Any dictionary will reveal that the terms popularly employed for the description of events in the behavior stream are not part of an operationally valid, internally consistent system of classification. Words in a dictionary are defined in terms of other words, not in terms of operations. This observation, of course, applies equally to all elements of a natural language, not merely those relating to behavior stream events. In the case of nonbehavioral events, however, considerable progress has been made, especially by physics and chemistry, toward the development of formal operationalized systems of units. But virtually no progress has been registered toward an operationalization of human behavior stream language by psychology and the social sciences. Indeed, this problem has received an almost total lack of attention.

In view of what has been said about the demonstrable value of common-sense behavior units, it may not be readily apparent why an operationalized set of units is needed. The inertia in this matter derives its strength precisely from the evident practicality of some common-sense descriptions of behavioral events. Since our newspapers, books, and daily conversations are replete with readily intelligible reports of what people do to each other or have done to them, why the urgency for a fresh approach to the units of the behavior stream?

There are many answers to this question, some of which are dictated by the abstract requirements of the scientific enterprise, and some of which are directly related to practical affairs. Certainly, every adult is aware that his natural language is an imperfect instrument. On occasion, we all misunderstand each other. Yet, for the most part, the deficiencies of natural language do not intrude themselves so long as discourse is confined to the contexts of experience to which the ordinary speaker is regularly exposed. But when the context is altered, when there is no longer a basis in common experience, common sense fails. Consider what happens when one seeks to describe the behavior of people whose learning experiences have little in common with that of the observer's community. Normal adult speakers of English understand each other fairly well when they report behavior stream events with the aid of terms like "cocktail party," "uncle," "family," "church service," "taxation," "buying," and the like. But it is another matter when we are confronted with the task of describing the behavior stream events of another culture. In this new context, the repertory of familiar behavior stream terms frequently fails to provide a coherent picture of behavioral events. Some of the familiar units occur, some are absent, and, above all, some have no words in the observer's language and are entirely foreign to anything he has seen or experienced. Under such circumstances, the lack of operational definitions of behavioral terms is keenly felt. When does a group of people having drinks constitute a "cocktail party" and when not? When is a man an "uncle" and not something else? What does "family" mean when a man has three wives and counts descent patrilineally? Is a Chukchee séance a church service? Does the Trobriand chief's acceptance of his brother-in-law's yams constitute taxation? Does the Thonga man "buy" his wife? Since none of these terms have ever been defined operationally in English, no clear-cut answer can be given to the question of whether or not similar behavior stream events occur among non-English-speaking peoples. The difficulty becomes grave in proportion to the number of cultures in which it is necessary to decide if it is the "same" or a different bit of the behavior stream which is at stake. For the purpose of testing cross-cultural hypotheses, the question, "How do I know that *X* bit of the behavior stream is present or absent in Cultures *a, b, c* . . . ?" acquires fundamental practical significance. The common-sense *ad hoc* adjustments no longer suffice. One must know beforehand what kinds of evidence will provide grounds for a positive or negative identification. Any other approach is a standing invitation to chaos and infinite nonsense. For when the criteria of "class identity" are permitted to expand and contract at whim, all proof or disproof must necessarily remain trivial.

The pragmatic value of common sense in some behavioral contexts, and its woeful inadequacy in others, conforms to the relationship between common sense and all fields of scientific inquiry. To achieve such practical results as sailing a canoe or quenching one's thirst, the common-sense term "water" denotes an eminently serviceable macrophysical entity in a time-proven fashion. But to construct a nuclear reactor in which heavy water is the moderator, it is no longer sufficient to know that water is a "clear, colorless, tasteless liquid which comes from the sky and collects in rivers and lakes."

Nor are the inadequacies of our natural language remedied by each and every substitution of a coined term for a vernacular one. One of the most debilitating vices of the behavioral sciences is the morbid fascination with jargon or expertise. These artificial languages intensify rather than cure the semantic afflictions associated with the behavior stream. Jargonization must not be confused, however, with operationalism. In a jargon, many syllables do the work of one, but all refer in circular fashion to dictionary meanings. To improve upon our natural terminological equipment, the new terms must in effect substitute replicable processes of observation for dictionary definitions.

The Classification of Body Parts and Motions

Let us return now to the field of inquiry, defined as the motion of the body parts or the "behavior" of all human beings. The development of a data language adequate for the description of this continuum is a matter of classification. By definition of the field of inquiry, two separate classificatory systems are needed initially. We must find a way to classify the parts of the body; and we must agree on the classification of the motions of the discriminated parts.

The difficulties associated with classifying these two dimensions of the behavior stream are not equal. In the case of the classification of body parts, the cultural anthropologist has readily available to him the systematic and intersubjective terminology of anatomy. Hence, I will not dwell upon the logico-empirical procedures which guarantee empirical status to the entities known as the human head, neck, arm, leg, foot, etc. The question of how many subdivisions of the major articulatory organs will ordinarily be specified in behavioral descriptions will be dealt with in a later section. For the moment, it seems reasonable to take the position that if one states that a man's arm, wrist, toe, or finger is in motion, all observers have access to a classificatory system which insures a maximum of intersubjectivity. But when it comes to specifying what kind of *motion* the head, arms, legs, etc. are executing, problems begin. If I say that John "raised his right hand," you know perfectly well what I mean by "John's right hand." But what I mean by the term "raised" is surrounded by a larger penumbra of doubt. "Raised" might simply mean that the hand's altitude relative to sea level was increased. But this increase in altitude might have involved a displacement of anywhere from a few inches to a few feet. Other displacements, forward, to the side, back and forth, might also have occurred. "Raised" tells us nothing about how fast the action was carried out. Another observer might just as well have reported that "John slowly lifted his hand to the shelf"; still another, that "John reached for the glass on the shelf."

CLASSIFICATION OF BODY MOTION: VECTORS

The most simple approach to the classification of the motions of body parts would seem to be one based upon the specification of the direction, velocity, and distance associated with the displacement in question. This strategy recommends itself by virtue of its promise of metric precision, but in other respects it is ill-suited for a science of the behavior stream. Basic response units represented by approximately equal displacements of body parts along linear vectors can be discerned readily enough. Moreover, some of these responses occur in larger compound units or chains, which are partially predictable, given the initial elements in the sequence. The chain of responses involved in walking, for example, can frequently be predicted, given the initial vector changes of the first step. But such a strategy would yield a very stunted science of human behavior, whose predictive powers would be meager compared with those achieved elsewhere in science. Merely to relate a bit of body motion to another bit of body motion in a closed, homogeneous system, would certainly not illuminate the conditions under which one performance rather than another takes place. By isolating the behavior stream from other events in the universe, we would in effect fatally inhibit the description of the relationship which exists between the organism and its environment.

CLASSIFICATION OF BODY MOTION: ENVIRONMENTAL EFFECTS

The fact that every motion of a body part is necessarily associated with some spatio-temporally contiguous and continuous alteration of things in the body's immediate environment opens up broader operational horizons. Such nonbehavioral events do not comprise part of our formally defined field of inquiry, but they must nonetheless be considered at an early stage in the development of classificatory procedures aimed at typing the body motions themselves. The use of environmental effect as a source of classificatory principle is suggested by the precedents of natural language, and is firmly established as part of the research strategy of experimental psychology. In the vernacular, we employ such behaviorally descriptive terms as "carry," "chip," "chop," "coil," to describe common incidents in the behavior stream. But these terms in themselves convey relatively little information about the motion of body parts. When we speak of an actor as carrying an object, we understand only that the designated bit of behavior involves the transposition of an object supported by some portion of the actor's body. We do not know, unless additional explication is made, whether the object was carried in the actor's hands, or on his head, back, chest, or neck. Similarly, the basic response in the Skinnerian version of behaviorism is the bit of behavior known as bar-pressing. The latter is an appropriate term if the bar is pressed by the rat's nose, head, total body, left paw, right paw, hind legs, etc.

Classification of behavior by focusing upon the environmental effects of the behavior needs no justification beyond that furnished by its obvious pragmatic utility. However, I feel obliged to point out why this classificatory strategy is in a deeper sense productive of a better data language. If we were to restrict ourselves to a data language based exclusively upon the specification of the motions of body parts, we would greatly impair our ability to describe the order which pervades the relationship between the organism and its environment. The fundamental nature of that order is determined by the fact that the organism can survive only if there is a feedback relationship between the motions of its body parts and certain alterations of the environment which we know to be essential for life. Thus all organisms must somehow or other transpose energy-rich bits of the environment into the precincts of their metabolic systems. Among the lower animals, this feedback tends to have a highly stereotyped, or ceremonialized character. Each instance of ingestion is very similar to all other instances of ingestion in terms of the sequence of body motions leading up to it. Organisms equipped with enlarged learning and memory circuits, however, display a great dissimilarity in eating incidents. In man, the diversity of body motion associated with similar environmental effect is greater than in any other organism.

Food is detached from the environment and moved toward the vicinity of the body by digging sticks and combines, baskets and box cars. It is put into the alimentary tract by chopsticks, forks, fingers, or saucers.

It should not be concluded that classification by effect precludes the use of criteria based upon body motion. It seems to me that we can advance to a practical data language only by striking a compromise between these two classificatory strategies. When a similar effect is achieved by a totally different set of articulatory organs, there ought to be some provision for modifying the classificatory status of the behavioral bit. On the other hand, we must not slavishly restrict our units to instances of pure body motion. Our basic behavioral units must, in short, avoid too deep a commitment in either direction; they need to consist of terms which convey some minimal information about the behavior stream in the narrow sense, as well as the important physical events which accompany the flow of the behavior stream.

NATURAL MINIMUM UNITS

In studying the effects of body motion upon the environment, which motions of which body parts and which environmental effects ought the observer to record? This question would be considerably less formidable if we knew that there was some natural minimum unit of response into which all body motions could be resolved without the possibility of further reduction. The epistemological reasons for rejecting this expectation have already been made clear. Each microscopic wiggle of a finger or a toe is a part of the behavior stream. When subjected to more refined observational techniques, the smallest part of a wiggle is found to blend in a continuous fashion with other wiggles. No matter how brief the moment of observation, a finger or toe is never completely at rest; there is always some motion, and hence a yet smaller bit of behavior, down to the level at which our instruments cease to give reliable discriminations. Nor is our problem lessened by concentrating upon the environmental effects. No matter how small the bit of body motion, some alteration of the environment is associated with it.

Failure to isolate natural minimum units need not be regarded as a fatal embarrassment. Atoms, once considered the indivisible building blocks of matter, have not ceased to be useful concepts now that physics has perfected instruments which detect a bewildering array of internal subatomic parts. The critical issue is not what are the smallest *natural* units, but rather what are the smallest scientifically *useful* units.

It should not be concluded that the search for minimum intersubjective units is in all other respects entirely devoid of direction. The situation is not quite that unstructured. Proper priority must be given to one of the operational principles previously enunciated, namely, that empirical entities are defined by the application of a particular measuring apparatus to a given field of inquiry. Unless the nature of the measuring apparatus is specified, the problem of identifying the smallest behavior stream entities cannot be solved. The problem will not automatically be resolved once this information is provided, but we will at least be able to state that the appropriate spatial and temporal body displacements lie somewhere within the limits set by our instrument's range. Of course, there is no reason why we must restrict our observational apparata to only one kind of instrument. We may use as many instruments as we have at our disposal. Each one poses a separate problem, however, and may be expected to yield data-language units of a variety peculiar to the instrument's qualities.

Ethnographic Measuring Instruments

I have driven the argument to this point with some reluctance, since the reader cannot but experience a sense of anticlimax in regard to what must necessarily follow. I have not invented, as you might perhaps reasonably expect, some new form of geiger counter or spectroscope intended to serve as the master instrument for the investigation of the behavior stream. Indeed, the instrument I propose as the basic research tool in behavioral studies cannot, in a strict physicalist sense, be regarded as a piece of observational apparatus at all. This instrument is the observer's eye. As a secondary piece of equipment, to be used in more restricted circumstances, I should like to put forward the observer's ear. And as tertiary apparata, to be used under yet more restricted occasions, I should like to propose the use of the observer's digital sense of touch and his olfactory receptors. Cameras, stopwatches, tapemeasures, balance scales, tape recorders, and pedometers may also prove useful for more refined analysis of the behavior stream. But these ought only to be employed after the observer's eyes and ears have been applied to the relevant portion of the field of inquiry.

Judged from the physicalist model of operationalism, the use of the unaided human senses appears to be an heretical departure. Almost all of the advances achieved by the sciences dealing with nonbehavioral events have been linked with the perfection of laboratory hardware. In the laboratory, the human senses are regarded as untrustworthy, inaccurate, and crude. The less they are depended upon, the better the experiment. Indeed, science has become identified with the study of phenomena by means of artificial sensory equipment and measuring apparata.

I hold this view of the naked senses to be unnecessarily restrictive. Laboratory instruments do not "improve" upon the human senses. Microscopes, geiger counters, and thermometers merely expose a cross-section of events which are the result of the peculiar mode of interaction between these instruments and the fields to which they are applied. The unaided senses provide data in their own right, which are similarly the resultant of an interaction of a particular sensory apparatus and a particular field of inquiry. Students of the human behavior stream need not apologize for a data language which is not the product of artificial sensory equipment and measuring devices. If we lack such an instrument, it is because our interest in the behavior stream lies in what our eyes see and our ears hear, not in what some conjectural apparatus sees or hears. Were we to invent a "behaviorometer," it could be nothing less than a homunculus.

The observer's eyes and ears may be regarded as natural measuring devices, which because of their evolutionary origins are singularly well-adapted to discovering pragmatically useful similarities and differences among behavior stream events. Although we do not ordinarily regard seeing or hearing as a process of measurement, there is actually ample justification for doing so. Any entity which is seen or heard is identified through its measurable properties, regardless of whether or not a formal statement of its dimensions is rendered in terms of standardized units. When we distinguish a dog from a rose, we are saying in effect that these entities and their parts have different linear and cubic dimensions, that they move with different velocities, and that they absorb different portions of the visible light spectrum. Moreover, despite the absence of formal metric standards, the unaided senses frequently achieve a degree of accuracy in combining complex, subtle, multivectored measurements superior to that of the finest precision-built instruments. The difference between a smile and a smirk involves displacements so minute as to defy measurement by artificial means. Yet, such distinctions, vital to successful adjustment, are made routinely by all properly enculturated adults.

Finally, it should be noted that ultimately even artificial measuring devices are at the mercy of the unaided natural senses. The results of an experiment must be read off from the pointers and communicated from one observer to another. Thus, the final product of most scientific operations consists of verbal or written signs whose decipherment is wholly entrusted to the naked senses. The efficacy of these marks or sound waves as communication media depends in practice entirely upon our ability to make metric or positional distinctions without formal calibration. This point has been succinctly stated by the philosopher, Felix Kaufman:

> It cannot be maintained that the subjective factors of sense perception are excluded by introducing measurable magnitudes. . . . Whatever self-registering instrument may be devised, there must always be a man using his eyes when he takes the pointer reading, which means that sense perception is not entirely excluded. (1958:37)

Thus, the proposal under discussion is not quite as heretical as it may seem. The efficiency with which human beings distinguish or generalize among written or spoken notations, musical tones, facial expressions, rates of approach of oncoming automobiles or pedestrians, and many other things requiring correct measurement for a successful and long life, suggests that the unaided senses are not incompatible with the operational model of empiricism.

Because of their lifelong preoccupation with human responses, human observers are potentially capable of identifying certain body part motions and environmental effects with a degree of intersubjectivity equal to that of reading a pointer on a dial or words in print. To be sure, the problem of achieving intersubjectivity cannot be resolved simply by giving the student of the human behavior stream free rein to report whatever he sees or hears. The contention being made is simply that there are *some* bits of body motion and environmental effects which can be readily discriminated in a uniform intersubjective way. There are other segments of the behavior stream which can be expected to elicit the widest variety of reactions among both trained and untrained observers. Our task is to identify the classes of behavior stream bits to which a high degree of intersubjectivity is attached, and to make these bits the referents of our data language.

I admit that the proposed measuring instruments fall short of the highest aspirations of science. But science ought not be regarded as an either/or activity. Obviously, there are degrees of being scientific which accord with the nature of the subject matter and the observer's technical resources. Cultural anthropologists need not be intimidated by the stricter operationalism of the physical sciences, and modern behaviorist animal psychology. Instrument-mediated measurement is, indeed, a desirable component of scientific activity; but it is not the alpha and omega of science.

3

The Smallest Cultural Things

On the basis of the foregoing discussion, it is now possible to give a preliminary description of the smallest category of behavior stream events suitable for the construction of a hierarchical meta-taxonomy of cultural parts:

1. The units must consist of a bit of body motion *and* an environmental effect produced by that motion.

2. Neither the environmental effect nor the body motion will be so small as to fall below an observer's naked visual or auditory thresholds.

3. All observers will agree that a particular unit has occurred when and only when it has occurred.

Actones

The term "actone," currently used in psychology (cf. Barker and Wright, 1955) as a label for very small or "molecular" behavior bits, will be used here as the name for the smallest cultural unit. However, in all except the connotation of smallness, the meaning of actone here defined will bear little resemblance to previous usages. These differences will be discussed in Chapter 7. In the meantime, my own definition remains incomplete. All that has been established so far is that an actone is a behavioral bit consisting of body motion and environmental effect which rise above the threshold of the observer's auditory and visual senses. Entities which the observer cannot hear or see will necessarily be excluded from the basic data language, although they may, at a later stage of analysis, be made the subject of special instrument-mediated studies. While the biologically controlled sensory threshold provides a rough but viable lower limit to the actone, there still remains an infinite array of possible spatio-temporal slices which may be taken above the visual and auditory sensory thresholds. Let us turn first to the problem of classifying the body motion components of the proposed actone units.

The Visual Observation of Body Motion

Obviously, we cannot initially be concerned with recording every visible displacement of every visible segment of the body during any time interval whatsoever. To achieve some semblance of operational uniformity, we must be able to instruct independent observers to watch similar parts of the body and to record similar displacements during similar time intervals.

Of the three elements in the visual observation of body motion—body part, displacement, and interval—body part is the easiest to control. As previously suggested, on the basis of vernacular terms which may readily be operationalized, the human body can be divided into a relatively small number of major articulatory segments: the head, neck, shoulders, arms, hands, trunk, hips, legs, and feet. This division provides some of the ingredients needed for two intersubjectively distinguishable visual "foci." The observer may record either the motions of the major segments themselves, or the motions of the additional articulatory segments which are anatomically subparts of the major segments—eyes, eyebrows, eyelids, nostrils, jaws, lips, elbows, upper and lower arms, wrists, fingers and finger joints, knees, upper and lower legs, ankles and toes. When the observer reports visible body motion in terms denoting the motions of a major articulatory segment, he may be said to be employing a *visual macrofocus.* When the terms denote the parts of these major articulatory segments, the observer may be said to be using a *visual microfocus.*

Neither the macro- nor microfocus need be employed to the exclusion of the other. The observer may change his focus as often as he wishes, as long as such shifts are publicly proclaimed. If the focus is not identified, two observers employing a visual procedure will obviously describe a single segment of the behavior stream as consisting of totally different events. On the macrolevel a locomoting actor may be reported as "walking," but on the microlevel he may be reported as licking his lips, blinking, and clenching his fist, in addition to moving his toes, ankles, lower and upper legs in the fashion characteristic of the bipedal gait. Since the behavior stream is an enormously complex phenomena, it would seem that as a practical observational rule visual descriptions of body motion should be carried out initially on the level of sustained macrofocus. One reason for this is that most macrofocus body motions can be associated with visible environmental effects, and hence lend themselves to the creation of actonic units. Many microfocus bits of body motion, on the other hand, are not easily associated with visible environmental effects.

Bounding the Actone

Let us observe an actor whose body parts are visually at rest. As we watch, a segment (macro or micro) begins to move. At what point in time and at what distance from the initial position ought we to regard the movement as terminated? We could decide arbitrarily that the motion is terminated when it has proceeded for one second, or has covered one inch, or whichever happens first. Possibly, a solution of this sort would lead to the discovery of some regularities. But these regularities would not, for the most part, be regularities of an actonic sort. This would result from the circumstance that an arbitrary spatio-temporal cut-off point for body action would most likely be associated with no visible environmental effect or with more than one visible environmental effect. Had the actor's hand begun to move toward a glass of water on a table several feet away, for example, every inch traversed would emerge as a unit, despite the fact that only during the last inch did an environmental effect become visible. The trouble with this strategy is that a visible environmental effect of body motion is no more likely to occur at one inch than at one half or one quarter of an inch. Nor is it much more likely to occur at one second than at a half, a quarter, or an eighth of a second. The strategy of an arbitrary spatio-temporal interval of observation would serve the requirements of intersubjective uniformity, but like other rigidly empiricist operations, it would sacrifice scope of knowledge for precision.

What other means are available for establishing a terminal point for a visible body motion? Since our smallest descriptive unit—the actone—is to consist of both a body motion and an environment effect, the possibility arises of considering the effect itself as the terminal point for the body motion. If this proves operationally feasible, then an actone could be defined as a behavior stream event beginning with the onset of a body motion and ending with the production of the first environmental effect caused by that motion. Of course, this maneuver makes the definition of an actone depend upon our ability to reach intersubjective agreement on the relationship between various classes of body motions and various classes of environmental effects. Let us turn therefore to the problem of defining and classifying the visible and audible consequences of body motions.

Environmental Effects

Environmental effects may be defined as any deformations or transpositions of objects in the actor's environment or any locomotions of the actor himself which are partially or wholly produced (or caused) by his visible body motion in conformity with known macrophysical laws. In relating a particular body motion to its effect upon the environment, the observer assumes that the effect would not have occurred at the precise moment of observation were it not for the immediately prior occurrence of some displacement of the actor's body parts. This assumption derives its validation from the observer's common-sense knowledge of macrophysical laws. In formal terms, these laws require that a change of position of a macrophysical entity be regulated by the physical forces acting upon it. If the observer is challenged to show how he knows that a particular motion of an actor's body is indeed responsible in a given case for a particular environmental change, he will ultimately be forced back upon the ontogenetic uncertainties of the inductive mode of reasoning. But it is not really our concern here how a particular physical cause and a particular physical effect are ontogenetically related. As long as the community of observers agree that the object on the table would not have moved as it did, when it did, without the intervention of the actor's hand, we may proceed to use the cause-effect relationship as a taxonomic principle. I believe such agreement can be achieved with a minimum amount of formal training, if it is not already guaranteed by common experience.

Effects Involving Other Actors

In dealing with the behavior stream, it is of paramount importance to distinguish between body ceremony which produces an effect upon the environment through the well-known laws of macrophysical motion, and effects produced by laws that pertain exclusively to the behavior field of inquiry and which have yet to be properly formulated. If the actor pushes a chair hard enough, it will visibly alter its position; similarly if he pushes a second actor hard enough, the latter will also alter his position. But whereas the chair will thereupon come to rest, the second actor may subsequently push back, swing his fists, laugh, cry, curse, shout, or run away. We are fairly confident that the pushing "caused" the chair to move and the actor to fall backwards, but we are not prepared initially to say that the push also caused the second actor to cry, curse, or whatever. The pushing and the second actor's falling backwards are bound together by well-known physical principles, but the pushing and the crying or cursing are related by unknown psycho-cultural principles which the observer's discipline is trying to formulate. For this reason, an actone ought never to consist of a bit of body motion in one actor and an effect upon a second actor for which the macrophysical laws of motion do not provide an adequate explanation, given the initial physical states of the actors.

Classification of Environmental Effect

Some body motions which produce visible or audible environmental effects are invisible because they are below visual threshold, or because they are obscured by opaque substances within the line of sight. But totally invisible body motions seldom have visible or audible environmental effects. Some exceptions do occur, however. Humming, for example, produces a distinctly audible environmental effect although no displacement of body part is discernible. Breathing, which may be invisible, sometimes produces a visible effect in the form of vapor on a cool surface. But these types of body-environment relationships seem to be quite rare, and need not concern us in the initial stages of data language construction.

On the other hand, visible body motion frequently produces visible and invisible, and audible and inaudible environmental effects in several different combinations.

Thus, for the observer employing both visual and auditory receptors, environmental effects fall into one of the following four categories:

1. Visible and audible (e. g., hammering an object).
2. Visible but inaudible (e. g., picking up an object).
3. Invisible but audible (e. g., humming).
4. Invisible and inaudible (e. g., emission of odors).

Actone construction might normally be concerned with all of these categories except the last. As a rule of thumb, the observer could concentrate upon visible effects, and give priority to their description whenever they were simultaneously accompanied by audible effects. But commonsense knowledge of the behavior stream leads us to ignore most behaviorally produced sounds, or to regard them as less appropriate for the data language than visible environmental effects. Justification for this attitude is to be found in the fact that most sounds which are a by-product of visible effects and are not part of a communication system rarely have important immediate physiological consequences for the organism. In its traffic with the inanimate environment, the human body could act in a completely soundless way without disturbing its essential life processes. In other words, if eating, drinking, locomoting, and copulating were carried out without audible by-products, a biologically viable adaptation would still be possible. Noisemaking—unlike pushing, pulling, or grasping—does not in itself usually bring the life-sustaining portion of the environment closer to the organism. Nor does it, by itself, usually keep the noxious parts of the environment at a distance. This is not to say that noise is biophysically inconsequential, but rather that its adaptively important biophysical results are achieved indirectly through processes which depend on psychological rather than physical principles; that is, through the influence of signs. Nonetheless, the possibility of carrying out ethnographic descriptions in which audible rather than visible effects would be emphasized should not be completely dismissed. Descriptions in which the emphasis is upon olfactory effects might also prove rewarding.

The Talking Actone

Since all human populations rely for their primary signal systems upon visible mouth motions which produce audible effects, special attention must be paid to all such sounds. From the point of view of actonic analysis, it will be convenient to regard all speech utterances as examples of a single actone, "talking." This actone begins with the visible sound-producing movement of the mouth (and the invisible speech organs) and ends when the mouth motion becomes invisible or the utterances inaudible. Both the "etic" transcription of the variations in the sound and the "emic" (meaning) analysis of the signals involve logico-empirical procedures that are independent of actonic notation and irrelevant to the actonic view of the behavior stream (see p. 137). The phoneme, the morpheme, the sentence, and the various syntactic categories of linguistic analysis may have analogues, as Pike (1955-60) has proposed, in the stream of nonverbal actones, but the data language of linguistic analysis is not suitable for the construction of actone-based higher-order categories. As we shall see (Chapter 8), the analogies require an epistemological stance alien to the empiricist observer-oriented operations, which provide the basis for the actonic approach. In the meantime, we may regard the verbal portions of the behavior stream as important events noted by the ethnographer, but temporarily separated from the rest of the behavior stream. The reasons for this strategy will emerge when the higher-order behavior-unit categories come under consideration.

Total Body Actones

Many clearly visible body motions result in no discernible alteration of the environment. People scratch themselves, lick their lips, blink their eyes, cross their knees, rub their hands, clench their fists, raise their eyebrows, point their fingers; and the effects of many of these actions are apparent only to the observer inside the skin. But in other cases, these bits of behavior carry information and form part of the population's communication system. None of these behavior events are accessible to actonic analysis, but insofar as body motions form part of the communication system, they may be treated in a manner analogous to that which has been proposed for the talking actone and verbal behavior in general (see Chapter 9).

Certain body motions which have no visible or audible environmental effect and which are not primarily part of the communication system do play a significant role in relating the organism to the physical environment. These motions result in a modification of the actor's position in relation to his surroundings and thereby set the stage for or modify the results of subsequent behavior. In the case of these *total body actones*, the movement of the articulatory segments will be considered the body motion, while the transposition of the total body will be considered the environmental effect. Walking, for example, involves a complicated series of motions of the feet, legs, hips, and arms. The environmental effect of walking is the modification of the actor's position. A similar analysis can be made of such additional total body actones as lying down, standing up, kneeling, running, hopping, and the like.

Simultaneous Actones

The behavior stream is frequently composed of actones which are performed simultaneously by more than one articulatory segment, and which achieve more than one simultaneous environmental effect. This is true in both mono- and multi-actor behavioral contexts. The most common variety of mono-actor simultaneous actones consists of nonverbal types accompanied by talking. However, many other varieties frequently occur, as when the hands and feet perform the walking actone, while also carrying or kicking and punching. Preliminary experience suggests that the number of simultaneous macro-actones which a given actor may emit does not normally tax the observer's ability to keep track of them. There is obviously a limit to the number of ways in which an organism can simultaneously interact with its environment.

But when the observer is confronted by a multi-actor situation, there will be many intervals during which he will be unable to note the actones of all the people within his field of vision. Recourse to a second or third observer and to motion picture cameras and tape recorders will solve part of this problem.

One should not presume, however, that the observer's task is to capture every actone in every observational interval. The primary intent of ethnographic studies is not to furnish a complete running account of all the actones in the human behavior stream, since very little scientific merit accrues to mere descriptive thoroughness. Rather, the observer is animated by special interests in some, but not all, of the types of actors in a multi-actor situation or in some, but not all, of the simultaneous actones which these actors are emitting. He is not equally interested in all that is happening, but is rather concerned with abstracting supra-actonic regularities of a sort which we have yet to conceptualize. The origin of these interests, and their implicit or explicit epistemological status, will not be discussed here.

At this point it should be stressed that the actonic approach to the behavior stream will not protect us from false hypotheses or trivial theories. False starts and wasted efforts are perfectly compatible with the strictest forms of operationalism. The actonic approach is not a method for generating true hypotheses, but rather a method for generating verifiable hypotheses. Statements about the behavior stream which lack an actonic base may be true, but there is no way to confirm or deny them. On the other hand, actone-based statements may be quite incomplete as far as the total behavior stream is concerned, but they at least have the merit of being susceptible to verification.

Toward an Actonemic Vocabulary[1]

Although many potential natural actonemes occur in the English lexicon, they are not syntactically significant, and are used indiscriminately along with other verbs in vulgar descriptions of human behavior. Also, like other verbs, they are used to describe both inanimate and nonhuman animate events. What we find are a series of words which vary in their degrees of fulfillment of actonemic status, ranging from close approximation to an artificial actoneme, to total actonic ambiguity. Consider the difference between *spit* and *push. To spit* is to eject a substance from one's mouth. The term is organ specific; one spits with and only with the mouth. *To push*, on the other hand, is to apply a force to some substance by means of an unspecified part of the body. One can push with his head, hands, shoulders, back, or feet.

Actonically empty or actonically ambiguous verbs in the English language far outnumber those which are actonically precise. Among the verbs of the former class, it is important to distinguish between those which are convertible into actonemes by the specification of body parts, and those which are irreparably alien to the actonic approach. *Push*, *pull*, *carry*, for example, can easily be converted into actonemes by specifying whether the action was done by the hands, back, shoulders, etc. But verbs such as *beautify*, *celebrate*, or *betray* imply an enormously complicated series of actonic performances and a level of analysis far beyond that appropriate to the smallest units of behavior.

I shall not attempt here to make an exhaustive list of actonemes. Preliminary experience suggests, however, that fewer than 100 terms are needed to describe a very high

[1] An "actoneme" is any term which denotes an actone class.

percentage of the actones in the global behavior stream. Some common actones may be roughly defined as follows:

ACTONEME	BODY PART	BODY MOTION	ENVIRON-MENTAL EFFECT
carry	hand	hand moves horizontally while fingers grasp	object moves horizontally
drink	mouth	mouth opens	liquid disappears inside mouth
drop	fingers	fingers open	object falls
pick up	hand	hand elevated while fingers grasp	object is raised
poke	hand	hand moves down rapidly, fingers grasping	object moves down rapidly
press (finger)	fingers	tips of fingers bend slowly	object compressed
press (palm)	hand	open hand lowered slowly	object compressed
pull	hand	hand moves toward actor while fingers grasp	object moves toward body
push	hand	hand moves away from body with fingers open	object moves away from body
put down	hand	hand lowered while fingers grasp	object is lowered

ACTONEME	BODY PART	BODY MOTION	ENVIRON-MENTAL EFFECT
rub	hand	hand moves back and forth, up or down, or circularly, fingers open	object is abraded and/or emits abrasive sound, or moves away from actor
shake	hand	hand moves rapidly up and down or back and forth, fingers grasping	object moves rapidly up and down or back and forth
sit	total body	lower to sitting position	total body actone
slap	hand	open hand moves rapidly in any direction	object emits loud sound and/or compressed
slash	hand	closed hand moves rapidly in any direction with fingers grasping	object moves rapidly
squeeze	fingers	thumb and fingers brought together	object compressed
stand	total body	rise to upright position	total body actone
stir	hand	hand moves circularly in horizontal plane, fingers grasping	object describes small circle

ACTONEME	BODY PART	BODY MOTION	ENVIRON-MENTAL EFFECT
throw	arm	arm moves rapidly, fingers open up	object moves rapidly out of hand
turn (finger)	fingers	fingers grasp and rotate	object rotates
turn (hand)	hand	hand flips over while fingers grasp	object rotates
walk	total body	locomotion	total body actone

Undoubtedly the reader will find many faults with these definitions. From the definitions as stated it is obviously impossible to achieve referential intersubjectivity. As a matter of fact, it follows from all that has been said about the inadequacy of vernacular terms for ethnographic description that no purely verbal description couched in vernacular terms will ever suffice to establish a vocabulary of minimal units. To prime an operationally valid descriptive system, one must begin with operations, not with dictionary definitions. This means that the class of referents denoted by any actoneme must be learned in common by a community of observers. Training in the discrimination of actones in sample situations is thus a necessary requisite for intersubjectivity—a requisite not only for ethnographic descriptions, but present in every discipline. Descriptive units of any sort cannot be standardized merely by verbal descriptions. Consider how intersubjectivity is achieved in the matter of metric measurements. No amount of words will suffice to create agreement about how long one meter is. The meaning of the term, "one meter," can be obtained only by the operation of marking off a distance equivalent to that indicated on the standard platinum-iridium bar housed at the International Bureau of Weights and Measures. In short, all scientifically valid units of measurements presume that the community of observers has learned the standard value of their descriptive units by learning to carry out similar operations.

What then is the value of the actonemic definitions listed above? I believe these verbal definitions to be useful, not for establishing immediate intersubjectivity, but for suggesting that intersubjectively valid actonemes can be developed. The body parts, motions, and environmental effects involved seem to me to be of that order of simplicity which is compatible with rapid learning by and effective dissemination among a large community of observers. Those social scientists who doubt that this can be done are surely in a greater methodological quandary than I, for if independent observers cannot be trained to agree on the difference between a push and a pull, we might as well give up the pretense of trying to be empirical about the behavior stream. Oddly enough, I suspect that many people who prefer to doubt that a push can be distinguished from a pull will not hesitate to compare capitalism with socialism, or the mind of Western Man with the ethos of the Orient.

LATERALITY

In the preceding definitions, laterality has been omitted as a criterion of body part. The assumption behind this omission has been that, unless one is specifically interested in studying the laterality habits of different populations, little is to be gained from the point of view of theory construction by specifying whether a push or a pull has been carried out with the left or right hand. In any event, from the point of view of notational accuracy, it is a simple matter to add the qualifiers *left* and *right* if laterality is germane to a particular hypothesis.

Actones as Universal Cultural Traits

Insofar as the ethnographer accepts an actonemic lexicon as part of his basic data language, he is committed to the position that the actones designated are not confined to the behavior of a single individual at a single instant. Actones, in other words, are classes of responses whose instances occur repeatedly among human beings. Inasmuch as actones represent such simple categories of behavior, we may expect that almost all of them will be found in the behavioral repertory of every human society. Thus, an actonemic lexicon amounts in effect to a list of the lowest-level operationally meaningful universal common denominators of human culture.

Of course, one may argue that a Tikopian does not push or pull, pick up or put down, walk or sit the way an American does. Birdwhistell (1952) insists that many simple body motions show patterned variations when exposed to "kinesic" analysis. He finds, for example, that some walkers "glide," while others "bump" or "bounce." But this argument, carried to its logical extreme, leads us back to the observation that no two entities are identical, and thereby effectively terminates our attempts to describe the behavior stream. At some point, one must decide that further discrimination of differences is irrelevant to theory building.

An Idio-actone Chain[2]

Actones follow each other in a never-ending stream, any arbitrary segment of which I shall call an idio-actone chain. A small chain which occurred one day went as follows: (1) walk, (2) push, (3) walk, (4) pick up, (5) pull, (6) pick up, (7) push, (8) put down, (9) put down, (10) finger turn, (11) put down, (12) finger turn, (13) pick up, (14) put down, (15) squeeze, (16) put down, (17) pick up, (18) shake, (19) spit, (20) put down, (21) pick up, (22) shake, (23) spit, (24) shake, (25) spit, (26) put down, (27) put down, (28) pick up, (29) put down, (30) pick up, (31) drink, (32) spit, (33) drink, (34) spit, (35) drink, (36) put down, (37) pick up, (38) pick up, (39) finger turn, (40) pull, (41) put down,

[2] An idio-actone is the observed, historical member of an actone class.

(42) push, (43) finger turn, (44) walk, (45) pull, (46) rub, (47) put down.

I hasten to assure the reader that his impatience with this treatment of the behavior stream has been anticipated and has its place within the strategy of the data language under development. A behavior record which consists of nothing but actones is not a very useful document. But I want to make it perfectly plain why this is the case, since vital methodological and conceptual issues hinge on our rejection of a pure actonic approach.

If we regard every idio-actone member of a class of actones as being the logico-empirical equivalent of every other idio-actone member of the class, certain segments of the above chain will obviously be found to recur quite often. Turning-pushing-pulling, etc. is probably a widely repeated sequence. On this basis certain higher-order nomothetic units of behavior might readily be discovered. But the trouble with such units is that they may be related to the environment in radically different ways. Hence our ability to predict and retrodict their occurrence must necessarily be very poor. Such a data language is scarcely worth the effort. The "same" actonic chain may be carried out with totally different kinds of actors, at different times and places, and the environmental effects may be rendered through or upon totally different portions of the environment. The reader may not have grasped that the actonic chain described above is derived from observing a bit of the behavior stream known as toothbrushing. More information must be supplied before such an identification can be made. We may conclude, therefore, that the search for recurrent behavior ought not to be carried out on the actone level. Behavior stream regularities need not be confined to actone chain recurrences. As we shall see in the next chapter, much more complicated sorts of recurrences can be identified if we are prepared to take the step of introducing additional classificatory criteria.

4

Stage Coordinates and Episodes

Common sense and actual ethnographic practice suggest that certain kinds of people emit certain kinds of actones in the presence of certain kinds of objects at certain times and places. The specification of actor-type, object-type, time, place, and actone results in the identification of a supra-actone regularity which I shall call an *episode*.[1] Actor-type, object-type, time, and place will be referred to as *stage coordinates*.

The introduction of stage coordinates vastly complicates the logico-empirical structure of ethnographic descriptions. The actone and the actone chain are now to be seen as merely one kind of ingredient in the basic data language. We may legitimately choose to confine our behavior stream descriptions to pure actone sequences, but

[1] This word is borrowed from Barker and Wright (1955). It will be convenient, as in the case of actones and idio-actones, to distinguish *episodes* from *idio-episodes,* the observed, historical members of the class.

we will do so only at the cost of limiting the resultant regularities to a very low grade of generality. The price for achieving a higher level of generality is a data language which is capable of designating stage coordinates as well as actones.

The specification of an actone's stage coordinates can be performed initially by supplying *absolute stage coordinates.* The latter identify the actone's actor, object, time, and place by means of criteria which separately as well as in conjunction are unique to the observational instant. Such absolute stage coordinates tell us that a particular person has emitted a given actone which involves a particular object at a particular moment in time and at a particular point in space. This kind of behavior stream event will be referred to as an *idio-episode.* The aim of our analysis is to progress from the idio-episode to the episode level. An episode exists only when a particular idio-episode is found in some sense to be similar to another idio-episode. To achieve this result, each of the absolute stage coordinates must be transformed into examples of classes of entities or relations. Thus, the actor must be identified as an example of a class of actors; the object must be identified as a member of a class of objects; the time must be identified as a type of moment rather than a nonrecurrent calendrical instant; and the place must be described as a kind of locality rather than as a unique point on the terrestrial grid. Such stage coordinates will be called *relative stage coordinates.*

Before examining stage coordinate classificatory procedures, it is worth noting how rapidly and inevitably we have been forced to expand our focus of attention from the behavior stream in the narrow sense to a field of inquiry which includes a substantial portion of the physical matrix of the environment. Once we have made the decision to go beyond mere body motion description, we are confronted with the necessity of classifying a not inconsiderable portion of the cosmos.

Actor-Types

The specification of actor-type answers the question: "Who has emitted this actone?" An absolute or idio-actor stage coordinate is furnished when this question is answered by designating a particular hominid in terms which directly or indirectly refer to an order of emergence from the womb of a parental female at a particular moment in cosmic time.

Quite a different form of response to the question, "Who did it?" is comprised by such terms as "little boy," a "policeman," an "old man," a "movie star," a "Jew," or a "priest." Here, the actor is identified not as an individual but as a member of a class of actors all of whom may be regarded as logically equivalent with respect to one or more criteria. In the vernacular, these criteria are seldom formally stated; hence, many of the commonly employed relative actor-types provoke interminable semantic confusion.

Two sources of relative actor-type criteria may be distinguished: (1) An actor may be identified by placing him in a class of actors based upon the fact that all members of the class perform some episode or higher-order unit of behavior in common. (2) An actor may be identified by referring to some nonbehavioral biological feature or relationship which the actor shares in common with other actors. An actor-type of the first sort will be called a *behavioral actor-type;* the second sort, a *physical actor-type.*

Behavioral actor-types are identified by classing together actors who emit similar actones, involving similar object types, at similar times and places. To prime the system, we may assume that initially the observer begins with the actor-type, "actor," and then proceeds to note that some, but not all, actors partake in certain episodes. For example, the following episode may be constructed: Sunday mornings (time) a class of actors (actor-type) pick up (actone) a chalice (actone object) in church (place-type). Following the vernacular lead, let us call this class of actors, "priests." Additional episodes may now be constructed in which the actor-type "priest" figures among the stage coordinates. Thus, we may note that chalice-raisers wear certain garments in church every Sunday morning and that they kneel and move from side to side before an altar. Of course, it may turn out that all Sunday-morning-chalice-raisers are also special garment-wearers-and-altar-kneelers-and-walkers. If so, "priest" may be redefined to include these additional episodic criteria. But it may be that not all chalice-raisers wear similar types of garments. In this sense, every episode implies the existence of a previously defined actor-type, and at the same time provides the material for the potential definition of a new behavior actor-type.

Relative physical actor-types may be constructed out of the great array of physical differences between human actors. Sex is one of the most obvious and important ways to classify people without appealing to actones. Similarly, age, measured in terms of precise age groups (five-year-olds, teen-agers, etc.), or by vaguer but nonetheless useful categories (infants, children, old people, etc.) may also be used to supply the actor-type coordinate of an episode. Body build (tall and short, fat and thin, etc.), skin color (light and dark, brown and black, etc.), hair color, eye color, hair form, and many other anthropometric and anthroposcopic indices may also be employed.

Of special interest are the physical actor-type criteria which stem from the observer's knowledge of the actor's biological genealogy. The "who" of a particular episode can be supplied by such genealogical terms as mother, father, brother, sister, and the like. Great care must be exercised in the use of such actor-type categories, however, since the vernacular English terms are notoriously imprecise. For one thing, strict separation must be maintained between kin-types which are part of the actors' verbal attempts to classify people, and kin-types which are strictly biological in nature and are based upon the observer's knowledge of actual genealogical connections. This distinction is by now well established among most professional observers and need not detain us further.

Recourse to genealogically defined actor-types usually implies a multi-actor situation in which at least two of the actors are genealogically related. Thus, it may be noted that a father in the presence of his son emits certain idio-episodes which are repeated by other fathers in the presence of their sons (for example, fathers' palmstriking of sons' buttocks); or that sons emit certain episodes in the presence of their mothers' brothers (for example, they run off with their mothers' brothers, *assegai*). However, genealogical actor-types may sometimes be employed in another fashion to denote categories of people who have or have not filled out the possibilities of genealogical relationships. Thus, we may note that males who have sired children emit special episodes (for example, they sit in a special place in the men's house), regardless of whether or not their children are present. One of the most important objectives of ethnographic research is to discover precisely what kinds of episodes fathers, mothers, grandparents, siblings, etc. perform in each other's presence, as well as what kinds of episodes they perform separately. As these episodes are identified, the observer progressively enlarges and refines the genealogically given physical actor-type categories. This results in the identification of relative actor-types whose diagnostics are partly physical and partly behavioral actor-type criteria.

In the construction of these operationalized actor-types, the verbal system by which the actors signal to and identify their demonstrated or stipulated kinsmen (their kinship terminologies) is not of immediate concern. This does not mean that the kinship terminology is unimportant, but merely that like all other forms of verbal behavior it must be given separate treatment. Certainly, it is a major consideration to determine the degree of correspondence between the actor's and the observer's classification of genealogical actor-types. All too frequently, however, the ethnographer contents himself with recording the kinship terminology and the actors' verbal statements about the behavior of kinsmen, neglecting the actual episodic content of the relevant actor-type categories.

Actor-types which are compounded out of physical and behavioral criteria are, of course, not confined to genealogical categories. The observer's development of compound types is limited only by their usefulness for the identification of episodic and higher-order regularities. Thus, we may legitimately speak of sisterless priests, red-haired policemen, or young, married, pregnant, toothless, lame, female, apprentice shamans, if these categories are associated with episodic regularities.

Actone Objects

Any class of entities which is moved or transformed by the body motion in an actone will be called an *actone object*. The unique individuals of this class are *idio-actone objects*. Classification of idio-actone objects may proceed along the two lines suggested for the classification of idio-actors: we may appeal either to certain physical and chemical properties of the idio-actone object; or to the common involvement of a number of idio-actone objects in similar behavioral units. Actone objects which are identified by their common physical and chemical properties will be called *physical actone objects*. Those which are identified on the basis of a prior inspection of behavior stream events will be called *behavior actone objects*. Compound actone object types, based partly on physical and partly on behavioral properties, should also be recognized, as in the case of actor-types.

Many of the actone objects which figure in the behavior stream can be denoted by vernacular terms based upon physical object classificatory principles. Common inorganic substances (water, snow, sand, rocks, iron ore), organic entities including live flora and fauna (dogs, elephants, cows, sheep, maize, barley, oak trees, orchids), organic derivatives (dung, humus, wood, resin), and parts of organisms (twigs, tree trunks, sheep eyes, lion skins, jawbones) can usually be specified with a fair degree of rigor simply by using the vernacular classification. If further precision is required, the ethnographer may invoke the established taxonomies of chemistry, botany, zoology, and mineralogy; or, for greater refinement, he may resort to physical and chemical analysis by measuring dimensions, weight, color, and chemical properties. Thus, every class of objects which is affected by body motion may in principle be defined by operations which are not based upon the observation of prior events in the behavior stream, regardless of whether or not the objects have previously been effected (or "manufactured") by behavior stream events.

Conversely, it is also theoretically possible to establish a taxonomy of objects relevant to the behavior stream without employing any reference to physical and chemical properties. A toothbrush may be defined as that object which is picked up, covered with toothpaste at one end, held to the teeth, and moved up and down against the teeth by certain actor-types at certain times and places. Only those physical object toothbrushes which figured in similar episodes would fall into the behavior-object toothbrush category. Behavior object classifications of trees, cows, or rocks could proceed along similar lines, with similar results.

In English, pure behavior object classifications are never employed. I do not know why this is so. Pure physical object types are quite common, however. The latter are usually confined to classes of things which up to the moment of observation have suffered relatively slight transpositions and deformations as a result of behavior stream events. The terms "raw materials" and "natural resources" connote the kinds of entities which enter into ethnographic descriptions as pure physical objects. Artifacts, or those things which have been radically affected by body motion prior to observation, are rarely defined as pure physical objects. Instead compound criteria are used. Our analysis should make it clear that any object which serves as an actone object stage coordinate may be considered an artifact insofar as it has necessarily been transposed or transformed to some visible or audible extent by the body motion acting upon it.

One of the greatest dilemmas of the ethnographic observer is the extent to which class criteria of artifacts should be rendered in formal operational terms. Vernacular categories of artifacts (knife, chair, door, book) usually imply compound actone object status, for which neither the physical nor the behavior object properties are formally specified. One is never quite sure whether a "knife" is an object with a very fine edge (physical actone object), or an object held in the hand which cuts other objects (behavior actone object). The vernacular term sooner or later becomes ambiguous, even when it is not applied cross-culturally. Thus, when we encounter an object in the shape of a kitchen knife, but made of soft rubber, or one made of steel, but never used in cutting episodes, agreement as to the definition of "knife" disappears.

Despite the obvious difficulties attached to the vernacular classification of artifacts, it is out of the question to expect rigorous compound physical and behavioral criteria to be supplied for every artifact employed as an actone object stage coordinate. Drawing up an operationalized list of such objects in an industrial society would require an army of workers. Even in a technologically retarded society, a full inventory of the material culture rendered in precise physical and chemical terms is probably unattainable.

In the face of this obstacle, our strategy cannot be to achieve a complete inventory of material items before entering upon the description of episodes. We must be prepared to proceed with a rather rough-and-ready preliminary classification of artifacts based upon vernacular usage. We must trust the observer's ability to distinguish between a chair and a table although he may lack criteria for distinguishing between various kinds of tables and chairs. When he reports that the actone object is an axe, we may feel confident that it is not a spoon. When he says it has a wooden handle, we may rest assured that it is not made out of steel. If he reports that the actor has picked up a wooden dish, we have no reason to suspect the object involved to be a ceramic bowl. If the actor opens a door, we shall not be told that he has opened a window. In other words, many, if not most, of the artifacts involved in the foreign behavior stream bear enough resemblance to vernacular categories of things to permit at least a preliminary identification of them in vernacular terms. As in the case of actor-types, endless refinement of the categories of actone object-types may be produced. The limiting principle is whether or not a particular refinement helps to identify an episodic regularity. Thus in toothbrushing episodes, the observer might choose to distinguish red lucite, curved, hard-bristled, six-row brushes. The only justification for doing so within the context of ethnography would be that the actors who employ the red brush regularly perform in some other episode in which green-handle users do not figure. In fact, the toothbrush is to be distinguished from other kinds of brushes only because by doing so we are able to identify episodes involving toothbrushes as having actones, relative actor-types, times, and places distinct from those associated with hairbrushes, shoebrushes, and floor-brushes.

It might be argued that insofar as some toothbrushes are red-handled and others green, or some ceramic pots are brown and others black, there must be some episodic regularity in the manufacturing process which is responsible for these distinctions. This may be so, but the ethnographer is not thereby charged with collecting every episode in the behavior stream. His study of toothbrushing episodes does not compel him to follow up all the episodes responsible for the production and distribution of different varieties of toothbrushes. Nor, when he is studying cooking episodes, is he compelled to investigate the manufacture of ceramic ware. The episode is a minor and very lowly element in the ethnographic edifice. The observer who is doing his job properly is not a dilettante collector of episodic bits. Rather, he is animated by higher-order hypotheses, rough theories, and hunches which arise out of common-sense experience and cross-cultural analogies.

A word of caution is in order with respect to the use of actor-types as actone object stage coordinates. Actones in which another actor is the actone-object occur only when the second actor is directly affected by pushing, pulling, or striking body motion. Under all other circumstances, actor-types cannot serve as actone object stage coordinates. The reason for this rule has been given in connection with the definition of the actone (pp. 40-41).

Note should also be made of the distinction between objects which are directly affected by body motion and those which are affected through physio-chemical causal sequence initiated by that motion. Obviously the effect of body motion is not always confined to merely the transformation or displacement of the actone object. Often, a given object is physically connected with additional objects in such a way as to produce a long chain of secondary effects when a particular sort of actone is emitted. When an actor turns a water faucet, for example, water runs out the spout and flows into the sink, down the drainpipe, into the sewers, and eventually out to sea. Thus, in describing a sequence of episodes, the observer is faced with the problem of how far he ought to pursue the chain of secondary environmental effects of tools and machines.

It is clearly impossible to expect each chain to be followed to its ultimate visible or audible link. If the actor turns the faucet, we do not expect to be told all the details of the water's journey to the sea. On the other hand, it may be descriptively useful to note that water has emerged from the faucet, especially if in subsequent episodes the water flowing from the faucet figures as an *actone object* or *place object*. Similarly, if an actor swings a hammer against a nail, it may or may not be of consequence for the construction of higher-order regularities to state whether the nail has entered into the material. If subsequent episodes do not require mention of the altered disposition of the nail, that secondary effect may be omitted. But if the actor later hangs a picture on the nail, the episodic record can be amended so as to make clear the connection between the nail which was hammered and the nail in the wall.

The construction of behavior stream regularities, however, is *not* at the mercy of how secondary environmental effects are treated. Regular sequences of higher-order units may be assumed to be associated with regular environmental effects insofar as the actone object, place object, and time coordinates are similar. The ethnographer's task is to identify episodic regularities; it is the task of the physicist, chemist, and engineer to explain the connection between the primary effect of the actone and the intricate trains of secondary effects which follow.

Place

Every idio-actone occurs at a definite point on or near the earth's surface. Such a point, designated by precise reference to the terrestrial navigational grid, will be called an *absolute place*. The localization of an actone by appeal to this absolute grid severely limits the chances of identifying recurrent portions of the behavior stream. As an alternative, we might consider the possibility of defining the locus of behavior in terms of a cube, rather than a point. Thus, we might locate an idio-actone by noting that it has occurred somewhere within latitudes 31 and 32 degrees north, longitudes 95 and 96 degrees, and altitudes 500 and 1000 feet above sea level. Any subsequent idio-actones occurring within this cubic space might then be considered as having the "same" place stage coordinate. But this procedure would not serve to distinguish many actones which, from another point of view, are occurring in different places, although still within the boundaries of the cube.

An actor smoking a cigarette in the subway, for example, is in a significant sense doing something different from an actor smoking a cigarette in the street, even though the actones, actor-types, behavior objects, and time are the "same," and despite the fact that they are separated by only twenty feet on the vertical dimension of a very small cube. Similarly, disrobing episodes merit separate classification in some cultures, depending on whether the behavior is located indoors or outdoors, or in certain rooms.

The principle behind such localizations as "in the house," "near the river," "in the subway," "on the roof," "under the trees," "in the sweat hut," is that place is denoted by proximity to a class of objects. The objects which provide the reference points will be called *place objects* to distinguish them from *actone objects*. It will be immediately apparent that a given class of objects may in one episode constitute an actone object and in another a place object. An actor may push a car (actone object), or sit in it, or walk near it (place object). An actor may sit down near his desk, or pound on it. He may stand near a river, or bend over and drink water from it. Actually, every object can be pushed, pulled, pounded, slapped, stamped on, blown upon, or in some way be made to produce an audible or visible effect. Moreover, every actone takes place near some object other than the one which is directly affected by the body motion. Hence, the potential of objects to serve both as actone and place objects is probably unlimited. It would appear to be unwise, therefore, to attempt to separate actone objects from place objects according to hard and fast physical, chemical, or geometric criteria. I prefer rather to separate them in terms of the following data-language syntactical rule: episodic stage coordinates remain incomplete unless at least two different objects (three, if we count the actor) are specified among the stage coordinates, one object being that which is moved or deformed by the body motion, and the other being that near, upon, within, above, or below which the actor is located. An actone object is thus to be distinguished from a place object by the role it plays in the observer's account of an episode. This in turn is set by the relationship of the actor and his body motion during a particular moment of observation. During subsequent observational intervals, the operational role of the "same" object may be reversed.

As in the case of actor-types and actone objects, place objects may be classified by physico-chemical or behavioral properties, or by combinations of both physico-chemical and behavioral criteria. A place object which is defined without reference to prior episodes is a *physical place object;* a place object whose classificatory diagnostics are based exclusively upon consideration of the episodes which occur in its vicinity is a *behavior place object.* An altar may be defined as a rectangular structure covered by a white cloth (physical place object), or as the object before which a priest kneels on Sunday morning (behavior place object).

Despite the theoretical interchangeability of actone and place objects, some entities lend themselves more readily to one category than another. Relatively small objects which can be picked up or easily moved about tend to be poor indicators of place; objects that are massive or are firmly fixed to the surface of the earth tend not to be affected by body motion and, hence, are relatively poor choices for actone objects.

Special attention is merited by massive objects into which actors frequently penetrate and which contain a stable configuration of a variety of smaller objects that are affected by body motion. Edifices or vehicles containing rooms and, of course, rooms themselves constitute ideal place stage coordinates. A house, barn, kitchen, office, railroad terminal, barber shop, bathroom, temple, canoe, or bus, when defined in terms of their physical form and the objects found within them, establish pragmatically useful loci.

Such place objects have an existence separate from the behavior taking place within them. Their identification depends not upon a prior knowledge of behavior, but upon their physical properties and the objects they contain. Behavior must be invoked initially only to the extent of noting that people frequently enter the object and emit actones within it. Subsequent study and classification of the behavior occurring within such places may be directed toward the definition of places which represent a compound of physical and behavioral criteria. But it is contrary to the fundamental requirements of an operationalized approach to suppose that an observer can rely upon a vernacular knowledge of the behavior occurring inside a bathroom to define both the bathroom and the behavior taking place within it. The observer who classifies a particular bit of behavior by the place in which it occurs, and the place in which it occurs by that "same" bit of behavior, is caught on the treadmill of tautology.[2]

As in the case of the other stage coordinates, place

[2] Barker and Wright in their use of the concept "behavior setting" appear to be on such a treadmill. They distinguish between the (very) rough equivalent of actone object (their "behavior object") and place object (their "nonpsychological milieu") on the grounds that in the former case the behavior is "circumjacent" to the objects, while in the latter, the objects are circumjacent to the behavior. Their behavior setting is a compound of "a standing pattern of behavior" which is associated with a particular nonpsychological milieu. "A person is seen to enter, to be included in, to be surrounded by a store, a picnic, or Thanksgiving Day, and the standing pattern of behavior occurs on the stage which is thus provided" (1955:9). But the source of knowledge about standing patterns of behavior is nowhere adequately explained. These behavior stream events are alleged to be obvious entities to the actors and, hence (mysteriously), to the observers. Nonetheless, they admit that "the basis of the perceptual unity of these behavior patterns is not clear" (p. 8). Apparently, we are to regard the 4-H Club picnic, Thanksgiving, The Methodist Ladies Aid Rummage Sale (p. 174), and the American Legion as primitive intersubjective givens. This amounts to a dismissal of the entire problem of the logico-empirical status of cultural things. Barker and Wright then proceed to lavish their efforts upon the identification of simple bits of behavior (their "episodes"), employing for this purpose the enormously complicated higher-level categories of "behavior settings," whose logico-empirical status is gratuitously regarded as firmly established, or unworthy of inquiry.

objects may be qualified indefinitely by the addition of more specific criteria. An actor may be located near a desk, but the desk may be in an office or a home, in the bedroom or the study, near the window or the fireplace, on the first or tenth floor. The house in which the desk is located may be near the railroad, or near the park which in turn may be near a swamp, or a river, or a hill. But by now it should be clear that no hard and fast rule can be supplied for limiting the amount of precision demanded of the observer. We cannot judge in abstract whether a particular specification of a place object is too precise or too vague. We must instead suspend final judgment until the higher-order units are brought forth and related to general cross-cultural propositions and hypotheses. As a rule of thumb, it would seem pragmatically most rewarding to expect the observer to locate each behavior stream event in terms of a place object which more or less surrounds the actor and which contains a number of additional objects in a stable configuration. Any place object containing or surrounding the actor and the actone objects will be called a *major place object. Minor place objects* are objects which are too small or too solid for the actor to enter with his whole body, but which, nonetheless, may prove useful for identifying behavioral regularities. A bathroom, for example, defined as an enclosure with a hinged door which contains a bathtub or shower, a sink, and a water closet, is a major place object. The bathtub, towel rack, medicine cabinet, shower curtain, sink, and bathmat, insofar as they are employed to impart greater precision to the place stage coordinate (e. g., "He stood on the bathmat in the bathroom"), are also admissible as place objects. Each major place object is, of course, surrounded partially or wholly by more or less concentric circles of larger and larger major place objects. The bathroom is in a house, the house is in a town, the town is in a valley. How many concentric major places and how many minor place objects ought to be stipulated in any one place stage coordinate is an entirely pragmatic issue dependent upon the interests of the ethnographer and the generalizations which are produced.

In classifying both major and minor place objects, the same care as that demanded by the classification of actor-types and actone objects must naturally be exercised to prevent the extension of vernacular categories into phenomenological domains which lie outside the vernacular range of denotation. If we are told that an event is taking place under a tree or in a field of wheat, we need not fear that it is really taking place inside a cave or in a rice paddy. On the other hand, if an observer reports on an event occurring in a sweat house or a kraal, he will presumably furnish a physical description of the objects involved in terms which reduce these foreign things to familiar physical place-object types.

Time

Just as every idio-actone occurs at a point in space which can be uniquely specified in terms of an absolute (macro-physically speaking) geometric grid, so too each idio-actone can be specified in terms of a unique moment in time. Behavior stream events may thus be referred to as occurring at different times, if, according to our on-going chronological record, they occurred at a different minute of a certain day of a certain year. This mode of locating an event in time (absolute time) is, of course, extremely useful in the applied sciences and in history. But it is not the kind of time reckoning which lends itself to the task of constructing behavior stream regularities. A moment of absolute time bears no resemblance to any other moment of absolute time, except insofar as one moment is longer or shorter, earlier or later than another with respect to some absolute reference date.

The "when" of a behavior stream event may be viewed from a different standpoint. Our concern need not be focused upon absolute chronology, but may instead locate an event in time by relating it to some recurrent events of a cyclical sort. For relative time, the diurnal and annual movements of the earth can be taken as providing the basis for all episodic time specifications. We may speak of an episode as occurring at 6:00 A.M., or between five and six o'clock in the morning, or afternoon, or evening, in the month of May or in October, every other day or once a week or twice a year. Other cyclical time markers may depend on regular meteorological, biological, and geophysical cycles which are indirectly related to the earth's astronomical cycles. For example, an episode may have the time stage coordinate high tide, rainy season, seed-time, spawning season, or monsoon season.

In the vernacular, the time of an episode is frequently reckoned by appealing to events which are not directly related to astronomical time. Upon inspection, most of these time specifications are actually reducible to place or actor-type stage coordinates. Consider the statement that a certain actone is emitted "when there is a rainbow in the sky," or "when the sea is calm," or "when the roof leaks." The "when" in such statements actually answers the question "where" since what is really being said is that the actone occurs at a spatial location from which a rainbow, or a calm sea, or a leaky roof is visible to the observer.

Other vernacular references to time turn out, upon examination, to represent a confusion between time and actor-type. Phrases such as, "when a man is married," "when a boy reaches adolescence," or "when a woman gets old," frequently conform to the criteria of actor-type rather than to the criteria of time. In many cases of this sort one can say "a married man," or "an adolescent boy," or "an old woman" without distorting the data. The latter forms of expression are preferable, of course, only as they may point up the absence of a genuine time coordinate in the description of the episode.

The time stage coordinate must also be distinguished from the time interval between actones, episodes, and higher-order units. For example, in describing the sequence of episodes in toothbrushing, we may report: "After the actor hand-squeezes the paste onto the brush, he picks up the brush." Here the term "after" does not constitute a specification of the time stage coordinate. It merely tells us that one episode occurs earlier than another, but the time coordinate of both episodes is left undefined. Naturally, the time-order sequence of actones, episodes, and higher-level units is of great importance in the description of behavior stream regularities. Only by knowing when one unit occurs in relation to another can we proceed to construct episodic and supra-episodic regularities. But all such regularities must be anchored in astronomical time, since episodic sequences which have similar actor-types, actone objects, place objects, and similar intervals separating the components, may have radically different time coordinates. Suppose we observe a man drinking two martinis early in the morning. We are not likely to regard the episodic sequence involved as being quite the "same" as an otherwise very similar performance early in the evening.

Episodes

The definition of an episode as an actone for which four stage coordinates have been supplied corresponds roughly to supplying answers to the questions, who, what, when, and where. Other than the fact that the episode is thus a descriptive unit which fulfills the standard mandate of good journalism, is there any justification for insisting on four and only four coordinates? Once again we are forced back to pragmatic considerations. There is no logical reason why actone + actor-type, or actone + place and time, or any other combination of coordinates may not be made the basis of higher-order abstractions. The only reason for insisting that the episode be standardized in relation to four coordinates is that it is known that nomothetic regularities can be identified which specify who, what, when, and where. By requiring four coordinates rather than some smaller number, we are in effect freighting all supra-actonic units with the raw material for the abstraction of a maximum degree of behavioral regularity. The possibility of constructing a meta-taxonomy of cultural things based upon a different set of stage coordinates remains worthy of investigation. But the essential point here is that the choice of coordinates must be made explicit, for the nature of higher-order cultural things will vary in accordance with the kind of selection made.

5

Episode Chains, Nodes, and Nodal Chains

We now approach the task of recording and analyzing the episodic content of the behavior stream. Any continuous sequence of idio-episodes will be called an *idio-episode chain.* Our initial concern will be with idio-episode chains emitted by single actors, momentarily postponing the question of multi-actor situations.

As an example of such a chain, consider the following idio-episodes which my wife kindly permitted me to record:[1]

[1] For notational and mnemonic convenience, I have specified the actone objects and place objects of each idio-episode by their vernacular nomenclature. Thus, the place objects—kitchen and house—have been employed rather than the lengthy physical description which might be required were we totally naive observers. The use of these terms and such additional ones as stove, knife, refrigerator, is compatible with the attempt to record the behavior stream events in a culture-free fashion. It would be relatively easy, though expensive, to submit scale drawings of these objects and then refer to them by an artificial nomenclature. We may proceed without that expedient if it is established that by the use of the vernacular terms nothing more than the equivalent of a set of drawings or

ACTOR-TYPE: *Adult Female*
PLACE: *Kitchen*
TIME: *Early Evening*

1. Walk to cabinet.
2. Pull drawer out.
3. Pick up knife.
4. Push drawer.
5a. Carry knife.
 b. Walk to refrigerator.
6. Pull refrigerator door.
7. Pick up 3 baked potatoes.
8. Push refrigerator door.
9a. Carry knife.
 b. Walk to table.
 c. Carry potatoes.
10a. Put down knife.
 b. Put down potatoes on table.
11. Walk to cabinet.
12. Pull door open.
13. Pick up frying pan.
14. Push door of cabinet.
15a. Walk to table.
 b. Carry frying pan.
16. Put down frying pan on table.
17. Sit down (next to table).
18. Pick up knife.
19. Pick up potato.
20. Pull knife under potato skin (skin falls on table).
21. Pull knife through skinless potato (slices fall into pan). Repeat with second and third potato.
22. Put down knife on table.
23. Pull garbage pail.
24. Push potato peels over edge of table (and into pail).
25a. Stand up.
 b. Pick up frying pan (with potato slices in it).
26a. Walk to stove.
 b. Carry frying pan.
27a. Finger turn burner control.
 b. Put down frying pan on stove burner.
28. Walk to cabinet.
29. Open drawer.

The most important question for an ethnographer as distinct from a psychologist or a historian, with respect to this or any other idio-episode chain, is whether or not

---

photographs of the designated objects is implied. To conserve space, the primary place coordinate has not been repeated for each idio-episode. Simultaneous idio-episodes are labeled "a," "b," "c," etc.

the enumerated idio-episodes are in some sense repeated by other actors. That portion of the behavior stream which is never replicated is of no interest to a science of culture.

It will be seen that the structure of the data language which has been employed automatically bestows upon the actonic portion of the record a nomothetic status. Thus, each pick up, put down, walk, carry, is an instance of an actone class presumed to have additional instances in every human population. It is an empirical question, however, whether the idio-episodes in an observed chain are instances of nomothetic classes. What we must look for is repetition of the idio-episodes in the behavior of several different actors.

In the case of the sample kitchen performance, the observer can easily establish the nomothetic status of each of the idio-episodes by watching additional early evening performances carried out by other female actors. Millions of American women undoubtedly pick up knives, put down plates, turn water faucets, walk to the stove, and carry butter dishes in kitchens in homes in the early evening. Indeed, it is highly probable that in any idio-episode chain of considerable length, the great majority of idio-episodes will have nomothetic facsimiles in the behavior of at least one other actor. Otherwise, we must suppose an extraordinary degree of inventive genius and rate of change in the behavioral repertory of a given population.

Assuming that the nomothetic status of the idio-episodes in a particular chain has been established, what procedures may be employed to determine if the chain itself in whole or part is ever replicated in the behavior of other actors? Here we confront the distressing fact that the sample episode chain under analysis is a fragment of a larger segment of behavior which in the complete record contains some 480 separate episodes. Moreover, it took only twenty minutes for these 480 behavior stream events to occur. If my wife's rate of behavior is roughly representative of that of other actors, we must be prepared to deal with an inventory of episodes produced at the rate of some 20,000 per sixteen-hour day, per actor. Of course, not all of these idio-episodes will be instances of different nomothetic classes; walking to the sink, for example, was repeated several times during the evening kitchen performance. Hence the total number of different nomothetic episodes represented by an idio-episode chain is usually somewhat less than the total number of idio-episodes actually observed. Still, in a population consisting of several hundred actor-types, the number of different episodes in the total repertory must amount to many millions during the course of an annual cycle.

The prodigious size of the episodic repertory of even relatively homogeneous human populations makes it imperative that the behavior record be exposed to further logical operations designed to yield units whose classificatory status is more abstract than that of the episode.

The Condensation of the Episodic Record

If viable ethnographies are to be written, the episodic record must be condensed. What is needed is some principle whereby certain episodes can be singled out as more significant than others, and whereby these episodes can be related to each other to form relatively short but significant chains.

At this point we come face to face with what I consider to be the major dilemma of ethnography. A choice among three options confronts us: (1) We may ignore the whole question by proceeding to emphasize those episodes which, for subjective, momentary, and undefined reasons, strike our fancy—an option which seems to have been adopted more often than any other. (2) We may try to solve the problem by systematically attempting to discover which episodes in the total record the actors themselves regard as most important. (3) We may seek to establish criteria of importance which do not depend upon the actors' judgments.

Insofar as there have been attempts on the part of social scientists to achieve a formal solution of our problem, the second option has enjoyed the greatest repute. The key concept employed is that of "purpose," "goal," or "meaning." The actor who has emitted a series of episodes is assumed to be striving to reach or achieve one or more goals. If these can be identified then the episode record can be replaced by the specification of the goals or by the linking together of only those episodes which contribute to the achievement of the respective goals. If the goal of the woman in the kitchen is to produce fried potatoes, for example, then a higher level of abstraction can be achieved by simply stating that she has prepared these artifacts, and that many other women in her society possess a similar trait in their behavioral repertory.

It is my contention that the principle behind the identification and use of goals for the construction of higher-order entities has never been, and probably never will be, coherently formulated. My objections are spelled out in later sections of this chapter and in Chapter 8. For the moment, let it suffice to say that there are at present no known operations by which *the* central purpose of a given actor's episodes can be extracted from the welter of criss-crossing drives and reinforcing stimuli which push and pull human beings through their daily routines. An individual's goals are usually multiple, often conflicting, and always inaccessible to direct observation. Merely to ask a person why he is performing a particular episode is of no avail, for no conceivable standards exist by which the whole true purpose can be disentangled from the false, partial, or consciously or unconsciously distorted purpose. Intersubjectivity in this option, in other words, is not even possible in theory, let alone in practice. Therefore, the key to the solution of our problem will be sought in the third option.

Only in the observer-oriented option is it possible to formulate a principle which can theoretically be made to yield systematic, intersubjective identifications and chains of significant episodes. Note that the argument for this third option as a generality, as well as the argument for the specific formulation which follows, rests primarily upon its *theoretical* possibility rather than its demonstrated practicality. In actual practice, the observer-oriented option cannot be carried out with step-by-step fidelity. This is so because the proposed principle involves a vast expenditure of man hours in order to achieve the analysis of relatively short segments of the behavior stream.

Why then, the reader may ask, is the third option considered superior to the second? Why bother to describe a scheme for condensing the behavior record when it is admittedly impractical?

At this juncture we must reflect further upon the three options confronting us. The first option constitutes the very negation of science. The second, if my view is correct, is theoretically inconsistent with intersubjective descriptions. This means that the search for goals, purposes, and meanings cannot be regarded as an attempt to approximate an ideal or model set of operations. It means that even with a maximum expenditure of research effort, one can get no closer to a resolution of the problem. In the third option, however, precisely because there is an ideal solution, one may speak of approximations toward or away from the operational model. To follow the third option is to follow an asymptotic path toward the perfect solution. The greater the labor input, the closer one can get to fulfilling the demands of the model. But in the second option, it is impossible to speak of getting closer or further away, regardless of the time and effort expended.

Thus the choice of the third option is not an arbitrary one, despite the fact that in actual practice the ethnographer cannot systematically carry out the specified operations.

Finally, it must be stressed that our understanding of the nature of cultural things is totally and unavoidably enmeshed in the decision to be actor-oriented or observer-oriented in our approach to the condensation of the episodic record. If we are trying to find the actors' goals, the nature of culture is one thing, regardless of whether we succeed in our attempt; if we are trying to find another entity, the nature of culture is something else again.

The Principle of Logico-physical Functional Requisites

A formal observer-oriented solution of the problem of extracting higher-order units from the continuous flow of episodes will be approached by postulating that some of the later episodes in a chain exhibit a logico-physical dependency upon certain antecedent episodes. This dependency is such that one may retrospectively assert, on the basis of simple logico-physical principles, that the later episodes could not have occurred unless the antecedent episodes had occurred. The relationship in question must at the outset be carefully distinguished from whatever necessary and sufficient causes may in fact be responsible for the emission of the chain in all its unique aspects. Thus, in the case of the kitchen performance, it seems quite justified to assert that episode 3—pick up knife—is logico-physically dependent upon episode 2—pull drawer out. But it cannot be asserted that the only way the actor could have gotten the knife was to open the drawer. It could have been removed from the drawer by sawing, burning, or blasting a hole through the top of the cabinet. Moreover, having opened the drawer—or having sawed, blasted, or burned a hole into it—there is no logico-physical reason why the knife would then be picked up.

The principle of logico-physical requisites merely asserts that the links of a given episode chain can be retrospectively assigned differential priorities which may hold true only for the single case in question.

To identify the logico-physical requisites in a sequence of events, is to say nothing about the conditions under which the sequence will or will not occur. Only after the sequence has become part of history—when all the other ways in which an event might have occurred are known to be irrelevant because they were not in fact part of the chain—can this special brand of logico-physical "necessity" be identified.

One might argue that each link in an episode chain is in some sense functionally dependent upon the entire set of antecedent links. Thus, in order to carry the knife away from the drawer (5a), there seems to be no *logico-physical* reason why closing the drawer (4) had to occur first. Yet, there may be a very strong *psychological* reason why, if the knife were to be carried away, the drawer must first be closed. But given the state of our knowledge of human behavior in general, and of the heuristically assumed state of ignorance with respect to American kitchen behavior, we cannot profess to any substantial knowledge about these psychological components of the episode chain. Indeed, it is this very ignorance which motivates our attempt to divide the behavior stream into operationally valid units. If we *knew* which links in the chain were psycho-functionally necessary, there would be no point in indulging in this methodological inquiry. But the fact is that we cannot relate the closing of the drawer and the carrying away of the knife to any well-established set of psychological principles. In the case of the logico-physical requisites, however, we do know that solid macro-objects cannot be penetrated by anything so large or so soft as a human hand. Given the structure of the kitchen cabinet, therefore, we know that either the drawer must be opened before the knife is removed, or that an access hole has to be created through which the hand can pass.

Nodes

Given any idio-episode chain, it is possible to inquire, with respect to each link, which links are its functional requisites. By counting the logico-physical requisites of each link, a graph may be plotted showing the rise and fall of antecedent requisites per idio-episode. Each peak of the curve represents an idio-episode which has required more antecedent links than its immediately antecedent or subsequent links. Such peaks will be called *nodes*.

The reckoning of logico-physical requisites will not contribute to an intersubjectively uniform identification of nodes unless certain procedural rules are formulated. The most important of these rules is that emphasis must be placed on inquiring whether a given movement or deformation of the *actone object* rather than the place object was dependent upon the antecedent links. It must be agreed that modifications brought about in the nature of place objects are not to be reckoned as a part of the nodal count until the place object figures in a subsequent episode as an actone object. For example, as a housewife slices potatoes over a frying pan, the behavior requisite for bringing the frying pan into position is not requisite for the environmental effects being suffered by the potatoes. But when the frying pan containing the sliced potatoes is picked up and carried to the stove, then the behavioral sequence responsible for placing the frying pan where the potatoes would fall into it is clearly a necessary condition for carrying the pan and potatoes to the stove. In other words the observer must eliminate all assumptions about the importance of place for subsequent behavior. Otherwise, place will sometimes figure as relevant and sometimes as irrelevant, depending on whether the observer thinks that the actor "intended" the episode to occur at a particular spot. An explication of certain additional rules of nodal counting and the nodal analysis of the sample kitchen performance are given in the Appendix.

Counting logico-physical functional requisites is a dull and time-consuming task. Yet once certain rules are agreed upon, there is nothing about the process itself which is theoretically incompatible with an operational approach. Someday it may be possible to employ computers to lighten the labor involved. In the meantime, it needs to be emphasized that absolute uniformity of count is not the measure of this operation's success. Some degree of variation must be expected from one analyst to another, espe-

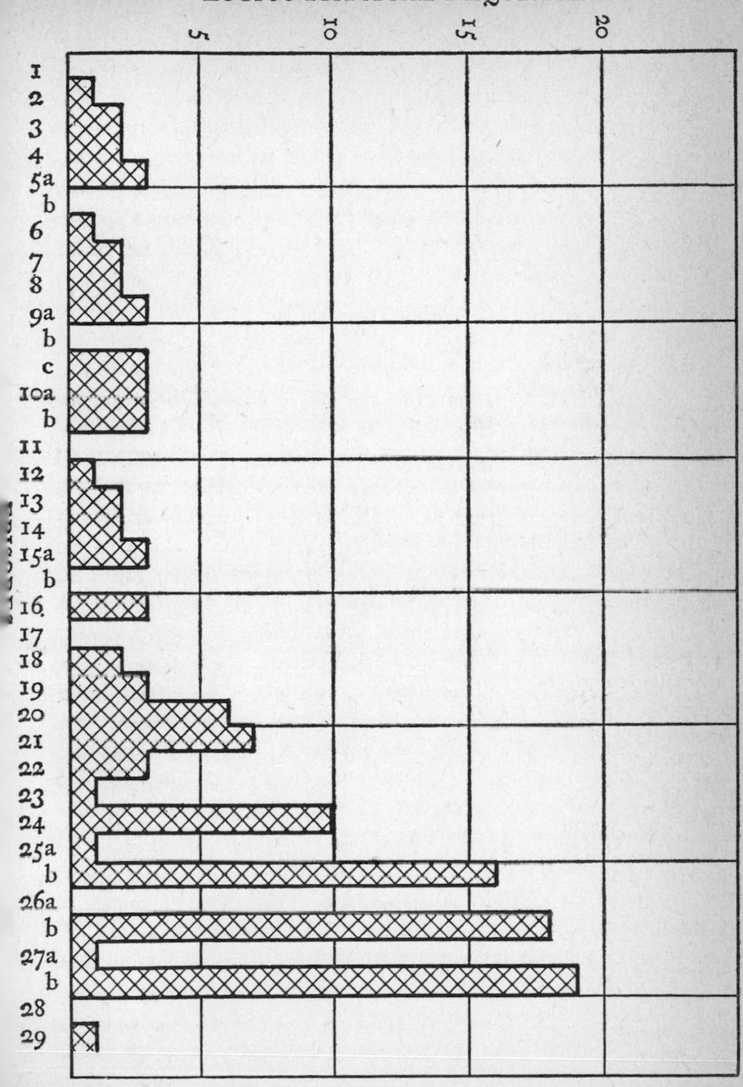
LOGICO-PHYSICAL REQUISITES
5
10
15
20
1
2
3
4
5a
b
6
7
8
9a
b
c
10a
b
11
12
13
14
15a
b
16
17
18
19
20
21
22
23
24
25a
b
26a
b
27a
b
28
29

cially when long chains are involved. But it is not the absolute height of the curve which is at stake here. What we are after are the relative peaks—the nodes—which indicate that the episode in question was, in an explicit sense, more significant than the average episode in the chain. This significance stems from its being relatively more dependent upon logico-physical antecedents than its immediately adjacent neighbors. Thus, even substantial variation in the absolute count would in many instances not change the location of the relative peaks.

Nodal Thresholds

The graph on page 81 shows that there are nine nodes in our sample of kitchen behavior. Approximately one hundred nodes occurred in the full record of 480 episodes. This means that systematic nodal analysis would reduce an episodic account of behavior by about ⅓ to ¼ of the raw total. While the reduction is welcome, it is not sufficient to alter the scale of our problem.

Further condensation could be achieved by setting an arbitrary level or threshold for the nodal count. Thus it might be decided that only those nodes having a count higher than 10 are relevant for the construction of higher level entities. In the fragment under study, a nodal threshold of 10 would reduce the 37 episodes to three (26b, 25b, and 27b). Higher values for the nodal threshold eliminate still more of the raw episodic content. It might even be appropriate in relation to certain problems to set the threshold at 20. At that level, one would be saying in effect that none of the episodes were "important" enough to form the basis for further abstractions. The setting of a nodal threshold is thus an operation which specifies the level of detail on which ethnographic description is to be carried out. It offers the theoretical possibility of stating in rather precise quantitative terms how fine or gross is the analytical mesh through which the episodic record is being screened.

Current ethnographic analysis depends to some extent upon operations roughly analogous to the formal notion of setting a nodal threshold. But in traditional data-processing techniques, the threshold is not explicit, and presumably varies from page to page and chapter to chapter in a completely irregular fashion. Ethnographers may one day be able to define explicitly the level of detail in which their accounts are written by specifying the nodal threshold which they have employed, but that day is obviously not close at hand. Yet once again, it must be stressed that the current impracticality of the ideal or pure operational model of a nodal threshold is not fatal to our exposition of the nature of cultural things. Nothing prevents us from approximating the model operations, even if we merely state that the nodal threshold has been set at a low, medium, or high level. This procedure is at least as intersubjective as the more conventional statement to the effect that a description has been rendered with or without attention to "detail." There may be no clear practical advantage in substituting a vague nodal count for an equally vague concept of "significant detail," but the former is clearly preferable, if our business is the definition of cultural things.

Nodal Chains

The principle of logico-physical requisites may also be used to achieve a formal solution of the problem of how to abstract higher-order chains from an episodic record. Given a condensed version of an episode chain in the form of a number of nodes, it is possible to inquire which of the nodes themselves are logico-physically dependent upon each other. Starting with the later nodes we can work backward, listing as part of an independent chain all those nodes which exhibit an unbroken thread of logico-physical dependency. Nodes related in this fashion will be called *nodal chains*.

I applied this operation to the full episodic record of

my wife's kitchen performance with gratifying results. At a nodal threshold of 6, five clearly separate nodal chains emerged out of the total of 480 episodes. The structure of the raw chains is diagrammed as follows, with time running from left to right, and with the relation of dependency indicated by an arrow.

Nodal Chains

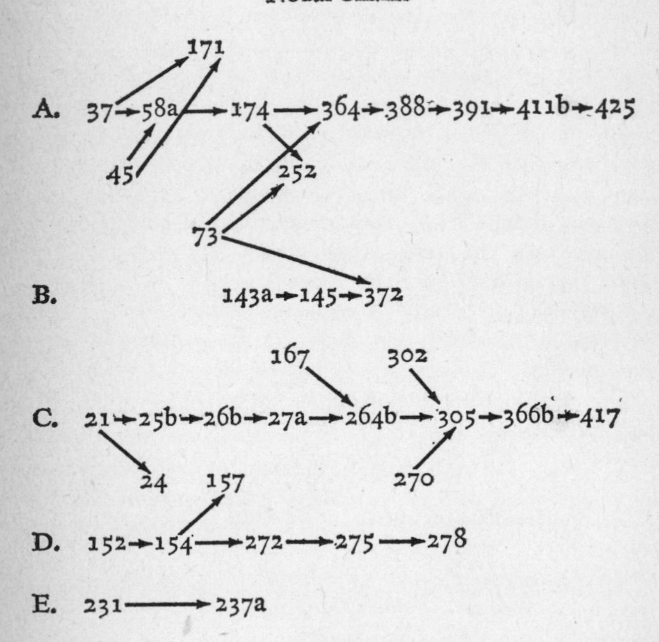

Note that the structure of these chains varies in complexity in accordance with the number of side chains which lead toward or away from the main thread. Chains *A* and *B* are a complex of many different side chains of varying length. For the task of nomothetic transcription, *A, B,* and *C* obviously require further processing. *D* and *E,* however, are structurally quite simple and might serve, with minor adjustments, as models for nomothetic units.

Chains *A*, *B*, and *C* can be broken down into a certain number of independent chains. Thus, in *A* we find:

$$\left.\begin{array}{l}37\\45\end{array}\right\} \rightarrow 171; \quad \left.\begin{array}{l}37\\45\end{array}\right\} \rightarrow 58a \rightarrow 174 \rightarrow 252; \; 73 \rightarrow 364 \rightarrow 388 \rightarrow$$

$$391 \rightarrow 411b \rightarrow 425.$$

In *B* and *C* we find:

$$73 \rightarrow 252; \; 73 \rightarrow 372; \; 143a \rightarrow 145 \rightarrow 372, \text{ etc.}$$

All of these chains are of potential interest. But in the absence of specific hypotheses, attention is naturally drawn to the longest chains. Those side chains, such as $\left.\begin{array}{l}37\\45\end{array}\right\} \rightarrow 171$ or $\left.\begin{array}{l}37\\45\end{array}\right\} \rightarrow 58a \rightarrow 174 \rightarrow 252$ which, as far as the later episodes in the behavior record are concerned, seem to be blind alleys, may be dropped from further consideration. Concentrating on the longest unbroken thread in *A*, we get the following structure:

$$\left.\begin{array}{l}37\\45\end{array}\right\} \rightarrow 58a \rightarrow 174 \rightarrow \underset{\nearrow 73}{364} \rightarrow 388 \rightarrow 391 \rightarrow 411b \rightarrow 425.$$

Reading back from my list of episodes, the idionodal chain in question turned out to be:

37. Finger press aluminum foil to form shallow tray.
45. Put down meat patty in foil tray.
58a. Carry broiler tray containing meat patty in foil tray to stove.
174. Push broiler tray containing meat patty, etc. into stove broiler compartment.
[73*]. Put down flaming match near oven lighter.

* I have placed 73 in brackets to indicate that the precise order of occurrence of the lighting of the oven in relationship to 37, 45, 58a, and 174 is ambiguous, since 73 is linked with several other side chains, but is not a prerequisite for any node in the chain under analysis until 364. Thus, we may say that a replicative instance of Chain *A* will feature a repetition of 73 at some point before 364.

364. Push in broiler tray with meat patty browned on one side.
388. Pull out broiler tray with meat patty browned on two sides.
391. Push in broiler tray containing patty with slice of cheese on top.
411b. Pull out broiler tray containing patty with melted cheese on top.
425. Shake spatula containing patty with melted cheese on top over plate (cheeseburger falls onto plate).

Our analysis has now advanced to the point where we could look for replicative instances of the idionodal chain, "cheeseburger making." Note: there is no reason to suppose that every feature of this behavioral event will be duplicated in the behavior of other actors. Some of the episodes may be omitted, or found in different sequence. Indeed, it might turn out that the entire chain is idiosyncratic (although this is unlikely).

It remains to be said that idionodal Chain *A* has been rendered throughout as if only one cheeseburger had been prepared, whereas in the actual performance five cheeseburgers were made. Obviously, the difference between making one and several cheeseburgers may in certain contexts be a significant datum. But in the present context we need not be concerned with this distinction as long as the structure of the idionodal chain is not significantly altered by the number of times certain episodes are repeated.

A similar situation confronts us in Chain *C*. Here, 167, 270, and 302 are essentially similar episodes having a common secondary effect: the adding of butter to a frying pan. Shall we insist that replicative instances can have three and only three episodes in which butter is added to the frying pan? Again, pragmatic considerations dominate. If there is no special reason for wanting to discriminate between a cook who adds butter twice or thrice, these parts of the nodal chain may be considered as replicated, despite wide fluctuations in the number of times they are repeated. Similarly, the number of potatoes handled, the number of slices into which they are cut, and the number of times they are turned may be ignored in the initial search for replicative instances. Chain *C* may thus be defined as follows, with 167 and 264b bracketed to indicate variable repetitions:

21. Pull knife through skinless potatoes (slices fall into pan).
25. Pick up frying pan with potato slices.
26. Carry frying pan.
27a. Put frying pan on stove burner.
[167]. Shake knife with butter slice on it over pan (butter falls in).
[264b]. Hand turn spatula under potatoes which have been browned on one side.
417. Shake spatula containing potatoes browned on both sides over napkin (potatoes fall off).

The remaining idionodal chains performed by my wife that evening were as follows:

B. [73]. Put down flaming match near oven lighter.
143a. Carry aluminum-foil-lined baking pan containing popovers to stove.
145. Put pan in oven.
372. Put down hot pan containing raised and browned popovers on wooden block.

D. 152. Hand turn open box of frozen stringbeans.
154. Shake box over pot of boiling water and salt.
272. Pick up pot containing water, salt, and stringbeans.
275. Hand turn pot (empty of water but containing stringbeans).

278. Put pot on stove.
E. 231. Pull knife across tomato.
237a. Put plate containing tomato slices on table.

Terminating the Idionodal Chain

The determination of the beginning of an idionodal chain poses no methodological problem—it is provided by the first episode which occurs in the series of functionally related episodes. But we have yet to describe how to identify an end to the chain. In the kitchen behavior under scrutiny, each of the chains was terminated simply because the record was cut off at an arbitrary point. As a matter of fact, additional idionodes occurred which were logico-physically dependent upon some or all of the elements of the nodal chains *A, B, C, D,* and *E.* This behavior in episodic terms involved, among other things, putting the cooked stringbeans and potatoes on the plates, the walking into the kitchen of two additional actors, the eating with forks of the stringbeans, cheeseburgers, and potatoes from the plates, and the carrying away of the plates from the table, etc. Is each of the nodal chains to be extended as long as logico-physical dependency can be demonstrated between the last recorded nodes and those which may later be discovered? There is nothing inherently wrong with such an approach, but it would be desirable only if the very long nodal chains, which would result, did not diminish the possibility of identifying replicative instances among other actors. Since we do not know *a priori* what degree of ceremonialization of the links in a nodal chain may be encountered in different idiographic stage settings and in different populations, excessive prolongation of the chain may result in failure to identify replicative instances, or in omission of certain regularities which would be exposed if chains of a shorter length were employed.

In the case under consideration, nodal chains *A, C,* and *D* actually join each other at a later point in the performance. This point is roughly marked by episodes occurring after the cheeseburgers, stringbeans, and potatoes had been placed on the same plates. In schematized fashion, the structure of this behavior may be diagrammed as follows:

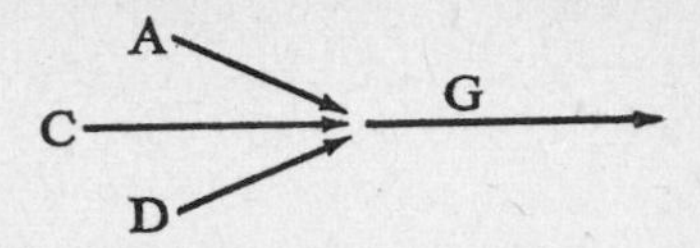

The question to be resolved is whether *A*, *C*, and *D* are to be treated as a single idionodal chain or as three separate idionodal chains. The question may be presented in the vernacular as an attempt to decide whether cooking food, serving it, eating it, and washing the dishes are to be regarded as single or multiple events. As a rule of thumb, the junction between *A*, *C*, *D*, and *G* appears to offer a pragmatically useful terminus for the nodal chains *A*, *C*, and *D*. In formal terms, wherever several side nodal chains, themselves of considerable length or complexity, meet to form an ongoing nodal chain, the junction may be taken as the nodal termini, until or unless the entire nodal chain system is found to be frequently replicated in all of its branches and junctions.

Idionodal chains, like all other idiographic events, are of no interest to the ethnographer unless they provide the basis for the construction of nomothetic units. If the sequence of episodes represented by the idionodal chain *A* is never repeated by any other actor, then *A* may be omitted from further consideration in ethnographic contexts. But in view of what is known about human behavior, it seems most unlikely that a nodal chain as long as *A* could be a specialty confined to only a single individual. An actor who can put together fifty or so episodes in a totally unique fashion must be regarded as either an inventive genius or a pathological deviant. On the other hand, there is little reason to suppose that all of the links in a chain collected at random will be replicated in an inclusive one-to-one fashion by additional actors. The links in a nodal chain are strung together along a thread of logico-physical dependency, but the precise concatenation is far from being fully predictable or retrodictible. Given one of the episodes, we may be able to predict with great success some of the others, but rarely will we be able to predict all of them. This means simply that each of the nodal episodes in the chain is part of an episodic repertory which is used over and over again to build many different chains. Thus, in addition to precise replication of *A*, we may expect to encounter other idiochains which contain all but one or two of the indicated nodal episodes. For example, an oven pilot light or an electric stove would eliminate episode 73 (flaming match to stove) —the omission of which would provide an empirical basis for regarding the second chain as a different entity. Yet, it would certainly remain our logical privilege to regard the two as similar by virtue of their sharing seven other episodes in common. The most important consideration in establishing nomothetic classes of nodal chains is not whether each instance of the class replicates precisely a given episodic content and structure, but whether the content and structure are unambiguously specified. We may insist that cooking on electric stoves differs from cooking on gas stoves, or we may insist that they are similar. This polemic can rise above triviality only if some hypothesis is contingent upon the distinction or lack of distinction. It is perfectly obvious that the repertory of nodal chains possessed by a given population must be astronomically huge. The ethnographer cannot record each and every idionodal sequence which has replicative instances. However, he can be expected to describe those chains which are emitted with greatest frequency by large segments of the population, which include a large number of episodes, and which are replicated with great fidelity of content and structure.

The Significance of Nodal Analysis

Quite obviously, the detailed analysis accorded the twenty minutes of sample behavior can be extended to the hundreds of hours of observation which constitute the ethnographer's usual tour of duty only by employing a huge staff of analysts. Budgetary limitations render this an unlikely prospect. But regardless of whether or not the step-by-step nodal count is performed by future ethnographers, nodal analysis does provide the solution to a fundamental epistemological problem. It gives us a model for an explicit, empirical technique for linking together separate portions of the behavior stream without invoking the actor's subjective understanding of what his "purpose" or "goal" is supposed to be.

As stated previously, the empiricist position demands a willingness to pare down one's primitive givens to a minimum. In the usual actor-oriented approach to higher-order behavior units, one is obliged to accept the primitive given that the actor himself knows the "purpose" or "meaning" of his behavior. In traditional ethnography, it is the actor himself who in effect establishes nodal thresholds, strings episodes together to form chains, and emphasizes some chains at the expense of others. Yet the assumptions implicit in this approach are totally alien to the spirit of science. The actor cannot join the community of observers unless he is capable of stating the operations by which he has been led to the knowledge of his "purpose."

That an actor regards a particular section of an episode chain as more important than another is a very poor foundation for cross-cultural comparison. Freud has taught us that the actor very frequently emphasizes precisely those aspects of his behavior which are psychodynamically least significant. Durkheim, along with Malthus and Marx, noted that the actor's "purpose" is frequently subsumed by a social "purpose" of which he is totally unaware. And recent anthropological studies have made clear that the actor cannot be trusted to analyze such higher-order units as feasts, conspicuous displays, and prestige hierarchies (cf. Harris, 1959). According to the actor-oriented approach the purpose of the famous Northwest Coast Indian give-away ceremony, the potlatch, was to put rival chiefs to shame. "The whole economic system of the Northwest Coast was bent to the service of this obsession," wrote Ruth Benedict (1934:193). But a radically different interpretation of the potlatch, emphasizing the redistribution of local food surpluses, has been developed using an observer-oriented approach (cf. Vayda, 1961; Suttles, 1960). Similar well-known discrepancies between actor and observer analysis might also be cited concerning head hunting, pig festivals, warfare, suicide, witchcraft, Latin American fiesta complexes, and the kula trade. One of the most striking cases of disparity between actor- and observer-oriented approaches is to be found in the Arthur Vidich and Joseph Bensman study of a small town in upstate New York:

> This disparity between public imagery and social realities put the field worker in an odd position. The familiar and indispensable sociological injunction to explore the meanings that social structures hold for people whose behavior they pattern, led them up a blind alley. Since the essential structural features of the community, through which its affairs are linked to the larger society, are not recognized by the participants, these structures cannot possibly hold any meaning for them. The local class system, the local political machine, the dominance of mass culture were all not only unrecognized, but when attention was called to them, their existence was vigorously denied by the very people involved. (Stein, 1959:209)

Nodal analysis challenges the dogma that human behavior stream events cannot be "understood" unless the observer attempts to unravel the actor's goals, motives, and inner "meanings." The actonic approach specifically denies that

> . . . the first responsibility of the anthropologist is to set down events as seen by the people he is studying. (Kluckhohn, 1949:300)

Whether or not episodes, nodes, and nodal chains are "meaningful" to the actor, they have meaning for the observer insofar as they represent regularly emitted and replicated behavior events which are functionally interdependent and involved in environmental feedback. In the following chapters I shall attempt to show that an observer-oriented approach is not only compatible with the identification of simple, low level units, but that structures of the most intricate and complex sort may be reared upon the foundations established by nodal analysis.

6

Higher Level and Multi-Actor Units

In this chapter we will move rapidly from the nodal chain level to the most abstract levels of behavior units. Cultural things called *scenes* will be abstracted from nodal chains, and entities called *serials* will be abstracted from scenes. It will be shown that nodal analysis is applicable to multi-actor situations, and that multi-actor equivalents of mono-actor nodal chains, scenes, and serials may be constructed without introducing new logico-empirical principles.

Scenes

In collecting data for the construction of episodes and nodal chains, the observer has the option of staying in a particular place and waiting for actors to appear, or of following a particular actor or group of actors as they move from place to place. In either case, the specification of place in terms of physical place objects is a prerequisite for supra-actonic constructions. Hence, a partial inventory of places must be achieved at an early stage of data collection. The elaboration of such an inventory can be guided initially by focusing upon places which are frequently entered by actors and are consequently rich in behavior stream events.

As behavior unfolds—in kitchens, verandas, stores, offices, village squares, sweat houses, or rice terraces—the physical criteria of place may be supplemented by behavioral criteria. The combination of physical and behavioral criteria results in the formation of a behavior stream unit which we will call a scene (nomothetic aspect) or idioscene (idiographic aspect). An idioscene begins when an actor enters a place, and ends when all the actors who have entered have left, that is, when behavior stream events are no longer happening.

The description of an idioscene may be carried out on an idio-episode or idionodal chain level. Every specification of an idio-episode, insofar as it must supply information about the behavior unfolding in a particular place, amounts to a partial description of an idioscene. Thus, each of the idio-episodes in a kitchen cooking performance may be regarded as a partial description of a kitchen idioscene.

For reasons previously stated, we can not be expected to construct an empirical nomothetic unit out of the total episodic sequence in an idioscene. In a totally ceremonialized population, each idioscene would be replicated by precise sequences of idio-episode chains emitted by definite numbers and kinds of actors. Since fortunately no such populations exist, the nomothetic translation of the idioscene into scene must be based upon segments of the idio-episode chain or upon idionodal chains. In the latter instance, it is not to be expected that each of the nodal chains will always recur, nor that those which do occur will maintain a fixed temporal relationship. For example, a kitchen scene in which the nodal chain, "making cheeseburgers," occurs, may or may not feature the chain "eating cheeseburgers," as when the cheeseburgers are served in the dining room. Conversely, cheeseburgers may be eaten in the kitchen without being cooked there, as when they are purchased in a drive-in and brought into the kitchen from the outside.

As an example of interactor scenic variability, consider the behavior which takes place in American bathrooms early in the morning. This scene appears to be highly ceremonialized on the nodal-chain level, but the repertory of nodal chains per actor and the order of emission of nodal chains per actor display considerable unpredictability. Ten informants were asked to check from a list of nodal chains those chains which they emitted when they first entered their bathrooms in the morning. The list of nodal chains was presented in vernacular terms, but the point being made here is adequately served by the responses obtained, since, if anything, the variability would be greater had the chains been given actonically precise definitions. The chains in question were the following:

1. Brush teeth.
2. Comb hair.
3. Wash hands.
4. Wash face.
5. Shave.
6. Urinate.
7. Defecate.
8. Take shower.
9. Dry hands.
10. Dry face.

The informants were asked to indicate the order of occurrence of these chains and to signify if any were emitted more than once. The results were as follows:

Variations in Nodal Chain Sequences

INFORMANTS:	I	II	III	IV	V	VI	VII	VIII	IX	X
	6	6	3	3	6	6	6	7	1	6
	1	3	4	4	3	4	7	6	2	3
	8	4	9	10	4	3	5	3	3	4
	10	10	10	9		9	4	1	4	5
	9	9	6	6		10	3	4	5	1
	4	2	8	7		5	9	10	6	2
	5		9	1		10	10	9	7	9
	4		10	4		9	2		8	10
	10		2	5		1	1		9	
	9		1	4		2			10	
	2			10						
				7						
				2						

From this list of nodal chains we can propose certain hypotheses, which of course would have to be confirmed by a more adequate sample. First, it seems useful to talk about early morning bathroom idioscenes since all of the actors did emit several nodal chains in that time and place. Moreover, logico-empirical grounds for the construction of a nomothetic scenic unit can be found, despite the fact that in each case the idioscenes differed both in nodal chain content and temporal sequence of nodal chains. Several options present themselves. We might choose to construct our scene on the basis of the two nodal chains (6) and (4), which occur in all cases. Or we might construct a different scene on the grounds that in 80 per cent of the cases (1), (2), (3), (4), (6), (9), and (10) occur. Or we might prefer to emphasize the order of occurrence and establish two types of scenes based upon whether they begin with (6) rather than some other nodal chain. Each of these options might possibly have some special pragmatic significance. It is conceivable, for example, that the actors who begin their early morning bathroom scene with (6) engage in other scenes, nodal chains, or episodes which are peculiar to them. From the standpoint of dental hygiene, those actors who brush their teeth before breakfast constitute a type well worth investigating. Similarly, since actor *V* appears to use a considerably smaller amount of water than the others, the construction of a scene consisting only of chains (6), (3), and (4) might be of special interest to a hydraulic engineer.

It is not necessary to regard nodal chains or sequences of nodal chains as the only source of scenic criteria. Fragments of episode chains, nodes, and even single episodes may be employed without diminishing the prospect of pragmatic significance. A perfectly valid kitchen scene might be identified merely by the episodes, "opening and closing refrigerator, pantries, and closets; picking up and putting down pots and dishes; and turning on stove burners." That a certain portion of the American adult female population engages in such scenes in the early evening is of considerable ethnographic interest even though none of the nodal regularities are specified. In fact, the mere presence of certain types of actors in certain places at certain times, signified by the emission of any actone whatsoever, may be a source of ethnographic enlightenment. When we report in the vernacular that John is "working" in the garden, or that Mary is "cooking" in the kitchen, we have in effect identified an idioscene by means of episodically empty concepts which nonetheless convey some information of potentially great ethnographic interest. We do not know what actones or episodes John and Mary are emitting, but we do know by inference that they are doing something in a particular place.

Very little is known about the degree to which the scenic repertory of various populations is ceremonialized. The impression persists that certain primitive religious performances are replicated with great fidelity, and that certain aspects of behavior in industrialized societies are highly stereotyped or regimented. Yet Robert Redfield's folk-urban hypothesis portrays the urban milieu as one in which a larger number of alternative patterns of behavior exists. Evidently it is perfectly possible to increase a population's scenic repertory while at the same time holding constant or even increasing the amount of ceremonialization per scene.

Multi-Actor Scenes

Although the congregation of several actors in a given place confronts the observer with a thorny tactical problem, the logico-empirical analysis of multi-actor behavior stream analysis does not differ fundamentally from that of mono-actor events. The bedrock data of a multi-actor scene consists of the actones emitted by each of the actors. These actones may be supplied with stage coordinates, and the resulting episodes may be subject to nodal analysis, which may lead finally to the construction of nodal chains. In theory, complete episodic descriptions of multi-actor idioscenes are perfectly feasible through the use of additional observers and the employment of cinematographic aids. Ideally, the transcript of such a scene would resemble a musical score—a separate line being devoted to the episodic chain being emitted by each actor, an over-all time grid indicating the respective temporal orders of emission of each episodic line, and denotations indicating entrance (↓) and exit (↑) from the scene:

Actors	Episodes
A.	(↓) 1 2 3 4 5 6 etc.
B.	(↓) 1 2 3 4 (↑)
C.	(↓) 1 2 3 4 5 6 7 8 9 etc.

The following fragment of a multi-actor idioscene may be taken as our model:

MAJOR PLACE: Subway kiosk

RELATIVE TIME: Saturday night

ACTOR-TYPES: *A.* An adult male

B. His girlfriend

C. A changewoman

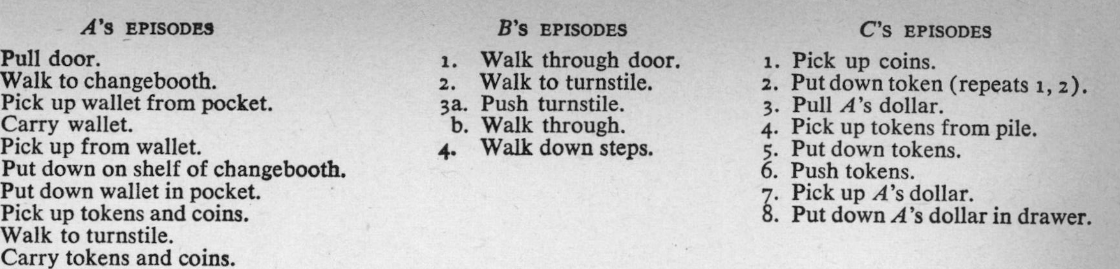

A's EPISODES

1. Pull door.
2a. Walk to changebooth.
 b. Pick up wallet from pocket.
 c. Carry wallet.
3. Pick up from wallet.
4. Put down on shelf of changebooth.
5. Put down wallet in pocket.
6. Pick up tokens and coins.
7a. Walk to turnstile.
 b. Carry tokens and coins.
8. Drop token in slot.
9. Drop token in slot.
10a. Push turnstile.
 b. Walk through.
 c. Carry tokens and coins.
11a. Put tokens and coins in pocket.
 b. Walk down steps.

B's EPISODES

1. Walk through door.
2. Walk to turnstile.
3a. Push turnstile.
 b. Walk through.
4. Walk down steps.

C's EPISODES

1. Pick up coins.
2. Put down token (repeats 1, 2).
3. Pull *A*'s dollar.
4. Pick up tokens from pile.
5. Put down tokens.
6. Push tokens.
7. Pick up *A*'s dollar.
8. Put down *A*'s dollar in drawer.

The score of this idioscene may be rendered as follows:

A. (↓) 1 2a 2b 2c 3 4 5 6 7a 7b 8 9 10a 10b 11a 11b (↑)

B. (↓) 1 2 3a 3b 4 (↑)

C. 1 2 1 2 1 2 1 2 1 2 1 3 4 5 6 7 8 1 2 1 2 1 2 1 2 1 2 1 2 1 2

Nodal Analysis of Multi-Actor Scenes

In multi-actor scenes, nodal analysis frequently reveals that a given episode has functional requisites in the behavior of several actors. These functional requisites may be included in the nodal count for each episodic line. Thus, while the nodes for each actor are counted separately, they are based upon the requisite behavior of all the actors in the scene.

The nodal count for the sample multi-actor scene fragment is as follows:

Actor A:

1. . . .
2a. A1
b. . . .
c. . . .
3. A2b
4. A3, A2b
5. A4, A3, A2b
6. C5, C4, A2a, A1
7a. A1
b. A6, C5, C4, A2a, A1
8. A7a, A7b, A6, C5, C4, A2a, A1
9. (repeat 8)
10a. A7a
b. A10a, A9, A7b, A6, C5, C4, A2a, A1
c. A6, C5, C4, A2a, A1
11a. A6, C5, C4, A2a, A1
b. A10b, A10a, A9, A7b, A7a, A6, C5, C4, A2a, A1

Actor B:

1. A1
2. B1, A1
3a. B2, B1, A1
b. B3a, B2, B1, A1
4. B3b, B3a, B2, B1, A1

Actor C:

1. . . .
2. C1
3. A4, A3, A2b, A2a, A1
4. . . .
5. C4
6. C5, C4
7. C3, A4, A2b, A2a, A1
8. C7, C3, A4, A2b, A2a, A1
1. . . .
2. C1

As a result of this count, nodes emerge on line A at episodes 6, 8, and 10b. There are no nodes on line B. On line C, 3 and 8 are nodes. Since A6 is a prerequisite for A8, and A8 is a prerequisite for A10b, we have the nodal chain A6—A8—A10b. On line B, since there are no nodes, there is no nodal chain. On line C, node C3 is a prerequisite for node C8, and hence we may construct the chain C3—C8. Assuming our interest to be in the analysis of the separate lines in the score, we could now describe the scene fragment in the following fashion:

A6. Pick up tokens from changebooth counter.
A8. Drop token in turnstile slot.
A10b. Walk through turnstile.
C3. Pull dollar into changebooth.
C8. Put dollar down in drawer.

A.		6	8	10b
C.	3		8	

Interaction Episodes

Our interest in multi-actor scenes need not be confined to the description of the behavior highlights as defined by the operations appropriate to the construction of nodal chains in mono-actor situations. In multi-actor situations, our interest may lie in highlighting relationships of logico-physical interdependence among the actors which are revealed by the nodal count. Of special interest are those episodes in the behavior of one actor without which an adjacent episode in the behavior of a second actor could not have occurred. I shall call these special episodes *interaction episodes*. All interaction episodes may be reduced to pairs consisting of the first dependent episode in the behavior of one actor, and the functionally prerequisite episode in the behavior of the second. In the kiosk scene fragment, the following pairs of interaction episodes are readily identifiable:

A1 → B1; A4 → C3; C5 → A6; A8 → B3b

Interaction Episode Chains

Referring back to our nodal count, it will be seen that some of the interaction episodes which belong to different pairs are the logico-physical requisites of each other. Thus B1 (walking through door) is dependent on A1 (pulling door) and is the functional requisite of B3b (walking through turnstile). By connecting all of the interaction episodes in the score with lines of logico-physical dependency, we arrive at the following synthesis of the events:

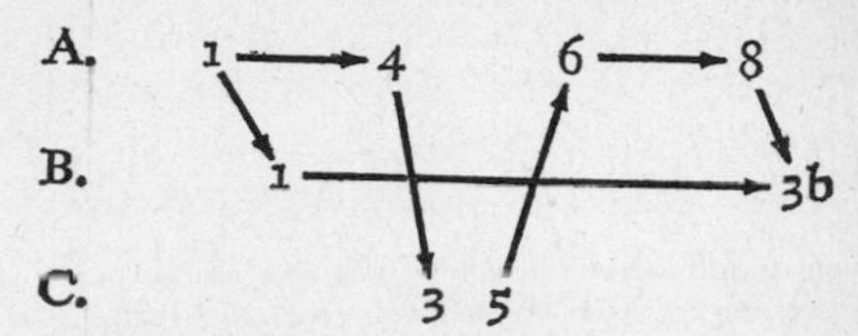

Reading from the score, the scene fragment may now be described as follows:

A pulls the door. *B* walks through the doorway. *A* puts down dollar on changebooth shelf. *C* pulls in dollar. *C* puts down tokens. *A* picks up tokens. *A* drops tokens in turnstile slot. *B* walks through turnstile.

Interaction Nodal Chain

An alternative treatment of the same idioscene fragment would be one which showed the relationship of nodes to nodes, interaction episodes to interaction episodes, and nodes to interaction episodes.

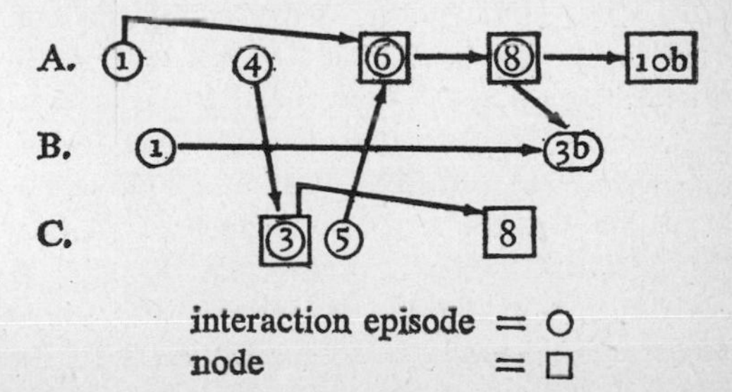

Our model for nomothetic translation may now be read as follows:

A pulls door. *B* walks through. *A* puts down dollar. *C* pulls in dollar. *C* puts down token. *A* picks up token. *C* puts down dollar in drawer. *A* drops token in turnstile slot. *B* walks through turnstile. *A* walks through turnstile.

Practical Implications

As in the case of mono-actor nodal analysis, the preceding discussion of multi-actor situations is not intended to be a literal step-by-step guide to ethnographic reporting. My concern here has been to show that, given sufficient time and personnel, multi-actor situations could be approached from a consistent observer-oriented point of view. In principle, nothing distinguishes multi-actor from mono-actor situations, except the possibility of recording interaction episodes, interaction nodes, and interaction nodal chains.

That one cannot seriously propose to carry out a step-by-step actonic analysis of complex multi-actor scenes does not mean that the foregoing operations are irrelevant to our understanding of the nature of cultural things. Indeed, it is absolutely essential for any definition of culture that some model set of operations for the analysis of multi-actor situations be provided. Failure to follow the model in all its intricate and laborious details is operationally preferable to having no model at all, or to having one which is in principle unoperationalizable. Our model does not prevent the ethnographer from taking various short cuts from the lowest level to the higher level units. In a complex multi-actor scene involving hundreds of persons, say, a fiesta in a Mexican village, some selective, classifying, and abstracting principle must be employed by anyone whose job it is to "tell what happened." It is of considerable practical import to know that the ethnographer has selected certain events and ignored others because some appeared to correspond roughly to very high nodal counts involving many interaction nodes among many different actors—shooting off rockets, carrying the image of the saint, feasting in the *carguero*'s house, etc.—regardless of whether or not a precise count has been taken. As suggested, emphasis upon an observer-oriented approach will in many critical cases lead to descriptions and interpretations of the behavior stream quite different from those emanating from an actor-orientation. But this disparity is not the main issue here. Our main interest is the nature of culture, an interest which can be satisfied only if we can tell how the ethnographer can break the continuum of the behavior stream, neglect some bits and some actors, and emphasize others. This interest is partially if not completely satisfied when one can specify the model or plan which the ethnographer approximates.

Serials

The analysis of pure behavior units can be carried to a level of abstraction one step beyond that of scenes. This can be achieved by linking together recurrent sequences of mono- and multi-actor scenes to form entities which I shall call *serials*. The latter do not represent the highest level of abstraction which can theoretically be achieved on the basis of the actone to scene hierarchy. But for reasons shortly to be made clear, I shall not push the meta-taxonomy beyond this level.

Linkage between scenes may be achieved in three ways:

(1). In a given place, one scene may follow another in a regular fashion. For example, each morning a very brief cleaning scene takes place in my office. The cleaning woman retires and the office remains devoid of behavior stream events. Later a new scene begins. A similar place-linked serial occurs in the household bathroom, as the respective members of the family enter and leave the precincts.

(2). A second type of linkage may be achieved by

concentrating on the actone objects rather than on the place. Fish brought to the beach by a fisherman, taken to the weighing hut by two little boys, put in a basket on a mule's back by a porter, taken to an icebox, put in a truck by the wholesaler, taken out of the truck by the truckdriver, put on a shelf by a retailer, and carried home by a housewife, link together a series of scenes whose actor-types and place coordinates are of the most diverse sorts. Extraordinarily long actone-object linked serials are associated with the processes of industrial manufacture and might well serve as the operationalized equivalent of the concepts, specialization, and division of labor.

(3). The third type of scene linkage is achieved by the continuity of personnel rather than place or object. The observer follows the fisherman rather than the fish. The fisherman regularly moves from his house to the beach, to his boat, to the fishing grounds, to the beach, to his house, etc. The housewife moves from the bedroom to the bathroom, to the kitchen, to the car, to the store, to the car, etc.

All three modes of scene linkage may serve to locate members of the population in a network of interlocking and cross-cutting serials. Of special interest in this network are the multi-actor scene, actor-linked serials. Such multi-actor scenes and serials provide the operational basis for the construction of a type of unit which is of central concern in the social sciences, namely, groups of actors who recurrently engage in interactive and interlinked behavior. As previously indicated, a helical relationship exists between the operations by which behavior actor-types are identified, and the further identification of behavior units. Groups of actors defined by multi-actor scenes and serials lead to the construction of additional mono- and multi-actor scenes and serials which in turn permit the construction of additional groups. We are thus inevitably forced to consider the problem of what kinds of groups of actors exist, for the ability to effectively describe multi-actor scenes and serials is in large measure the ability to identify the actors in terms of their group membership.

In this book I have elected to present a taxonomy of behavior units first, and a taxonomy of group units second. But the order might well have been reversed, since neither is fully intelligible without the other.

7

Groups

Great ambiguity surrounds the use of the term "group" in the literature of the social sciences. One of the rewards of the actonic approach is that it permits us to construct a meta-taxonomy of groups by referring to the behavioral entities which have previously been defined. Episodes, nodes, nodal chains, mono- and multi-actor scenes and serials in both their nomothetic and idiographic aspects, all lead directly to the construction of operationally valid groups. This result is opposed to a considerable body of social science doctrine which regards a "cultural" or behavioral data language as independent of the data language appropriate to the study of "groups," "social relations," "society," or "social structure."[1]

I do not mean to assert that a taxonomy of groups must necessarily employ the behavioral data language under discussion. Some kinds of groups can be established without any reference to behavior stream events. But this

[1] For influential statements of this position, see Evans-Pritchard (1951:17), Fortes (1953), Firth (1951), and Radcliffe-Brown (1952:190).

option cannot be consistently exercised without drastically stultifying the data language. On the other hand, all of the semivernacular kinds of groups, traditionally of central concern to the social sciences, can be shown to be dependent upon a data language of behavior units. Because of this relationship, it is utterly mischievous to propose that the analysis of behavior stream events may be optionally approached through the study of groups, or the study of behavior. Subtract information about groups from information about behavior, or vice versa, and what is left is equally useless. Those who argue that "society," "social structure," "social relations," or "groupings" can be studied independently of "culture," "customs," or "habits" are victims of a wholly capricious and meaningless play on words, made possible only by the failure of social science to develop an operational model of cultural things.

Here the term *group* will be used to denote in its primitive and most general sense a logico-empirical class of actors (human beings). As in all taxonomic enterprise, the choice of classificatory criteria for the construction of groups is devoid of natural limitations. However, a number of logically exclusive taxonomic approaches may be indicated. First, it is certainly possible to classify people without reference to their behavior. This can be done, as indicated in the discussion of actor-types, by using physical or biological indices. Thus we may speak of the group of red-haired New Yorkers, six-foot Japanese, or two-year old females. Secondly, we may classify people by reference to their behavior so that none of the group criteria involve the specification of any physical or biological attributes of the class members (e.g. thieves, students, liars). And thirdly, we may elaborate group criteria which specify both behavioral and biophysical diagnostics (e.g. father, Negro, prince). The ethnographer is legitimately concerned with all three kinds of group classifiers. But to demonstrate the relevance of behavior units to a meta-taxonomy of groups, I shall stress the non-biophysical criteria.

Paragroups versus Endogroups

Any behaviorally defined group, whose members never meet or participate in a common multi-actor scene, will be called a *paragroup*. "Potters," "farmers," "miners," "herders," "barbers," etc. can be interpreted as referring to paragroups. In contrast, there exists another fundamental kind of group which is distinguished by joint participation of a definite number of specific individuals in some particular multi-actor idioscene. Any group of this sort will be called an *endogroup*. All the members of a given endogroup may be members of one or more paragroups in common. Thus barbers Harry, Joe, and Vic in the "College Barbershop" constitute an endogroup characterized by their joint participation in daily haircutting scenes. But they are also members of the barber paragroup which includes an indeterminate number of actors who cut hair in barbershops throughout the country.

Paragroups consist of an unknown total of actors, while endogroups contain a definite number of specific individuals. Paragroups are composed of people some of whom the observer has never seen or heard: but in order to specify an endogroup, he must know exactly which members of the population are involved. A given paragroup, in short, continues to be the same paragroup throughout all increments or decrements of personnel. New actors may cut hair in barbershops throughout the country, and old barbers retire, but the barber paragroup is the "same" paragroup as long as the scenic criteria of membership continue to be repeated.[2] Of course, it is possible to inquire with respect to any moment in time how many barbers, or miners, or policemen there are in

[2] The concept of paragroup is closely related to actor-type and would be synonymous with it were all actor-types derived from behavioral criteria. Thus, male, female, six-footers, and children are actor-types, but not paragroups. In other words, paragroups are actor-types defined according to some behavioral event, in a manner which does not depend upon knowing whether all the actors involved meet in a common multi-actor idioscene.

a given population. Paragroups in this sense can always be represented by a definite number of real live people. But, each of one hundred barbers is no less a barber than each of one thousand barbers. The essential feature of the Harry, Joe, and Vic endogroup, however, is that it consists of just these three people.

Behavior Units and Paragroups

Every replication of an idio-episode by another actor provides the basis for identification of a paragroup. Such a group is a class of people whose members perform idio-episode instances of a given episode. All those actors who pick up a pot in the early evening may be said to be members of a pot-picking-up group; just as all those who pick up a toothbrush in the early morning may be said to be members of a toothbrush-picking-up group, or as those who put tokens in turnstiles may be said to belong to that episodically-defined category.

The trouble with paragroups defined in this manner is that, with a repertory of several million episodes in a population of only a few hundred people, we can expect to encounter several million different paragroups. Episodes, because they are so close to the universal actonic units, afford slight powers of discrimination of paragroups. Hence, we are compelled in the case of behavior-defined groups, as in the case of the behavior units themselves, to seek higher-order abstractions. Obviously it is of negligible scientific value to know that a class of people will emit a single episode in a given place and time. The more episodes we can predict for them (which are not shared by the entire population), the greater the rationale for picking them out as a special paragroup, and the closer the approximation to the scientific model. But it ought not to be concluded that paragroups whose membership is based on emission of a single common episode are entirely devoid of value. To know, for example, that all members of a paragroup have stuck a knife into a living human body, or that they have jumped from tops of palm trees, or walked on a high wire, or performed some other episode which is shared by a very small segment of the population, is to have opened the way toward fruitful problems of both an intra- and inter-population nature. We may inquire, for instance, whether the behavioral repertory of the paragroup members features additional behavior units—from episodes to serials—which are more frequently or absolutely associated with the group in question rather than with other paragroups. Turning outside of the population, we may inquire whether the paragroups are duplicated elsewhere, and if so, whether or not the additional behavior peculiar to them is also to be found.

This task is more efficiently and elegantly accomplished when the groups under study are defined by nodal chains, scenes, and serials, rather than by single episodes or sets of unrelated episodes. On the nodal chain level, for example, the operational equivalents of the vernacular labor specializations are readily discriminated. There emerge the paragroups whose members emit nodal chains related to the cutting of hair, the shaping and baking of clay, the mining of ores, the transportation of materials, the operation of machines, the carving of wood, the planting of seeds, the herding of animals, the painting of canvases. Thus the groups called barbers, potters, farmers, miners, or painters can be adequately operationalized by reference to their respective distinct repertories of nodal chains.

Paragroups may also be established by reference to both mono- and multi-actor scenes and serials. Thus we may speak of paragroups whose members participate in church ceremonies, cocktail parties, college seminars, puberty schools, harvests, or markets.

The most important point to be made here is that paragroups arise as an automatic consequence of the construction of episodes, nodes, scenes, and serials. The identification of these nomothetic behavior units signifies the repetition by two or more sets of one or more actors of certain behavioral events. Hence the number of paragroups which may be distinguished in a given population is potentially exactly equal to the number of episodes, nodal chains, scenes, and serials.

Endogroups: Idioclones

Unlike paragroups, endogroups cannot be specified by appeal to mono-actor behavior units. An endogroup is by definition a class of people who partake in at least one *multi*-actor idioscene. All of the people who perform in a given multi-actor idioscene or a given multi-actor idioserial have something significantly in common, namely, they have all participated in the given idioscene(s). Thus all people who congregate in a particular church on a particular occasion constitute a particular endogroup. Similarly, the members of a particular harvest work party, or the people at a particular football game, constitute a special class of actors—and so it is with any occurrence of a multi-actor idioscene or idioserial, whether in a fishing boat, a subway car, a kitchen, or a puberty hut. I shall call the type of endogroup distinguished in this fashion an *idioclone*. Note that an idioclone is necessarily associated with every multi-actor idioscene. Note too that the number of endogroups in a given population is thus potentially exactly equal to the number of multi-actor idioscenes.

Endogroups: Nomoclones

The existence of a given idioclone implies the existence of a multi-actor idioscene, and vice versa. The ethnographer is thus presented with two options for nomothetic translation. On the one hand, he may inquire if the multi-actor idioscene is ever replicated; or he may inquire if the idioclone is ever replicated. Consider a multi-actor idioscene in a subway car. If the observer enters a car during rush hour, he will observe a fragment of a multi-actor idioscene, defined by such episodes as pushing, elbowing, strap-hanging, book-carrying, newspaper-reading, etc. A properly naive observer would wonder if the idioscene he is watching is ever repeated. To find out he need merely get off at the next stop and enter the next train that comes along. Once again he will observe the pushing, elbowing, strap-hanging, etc.; he may therefore conclude that there are logico-empirical grounds for the construction of a nomothetic entity, namely, a multi-actor scene to be called "crowded subway car." Note also that he would have simultaneously constructed a para-group, consisting of all those actors whom he actually observed in the two idioscenes, plus all those actors who may participate in similar idioscene fragments which he did not observe.

Instead of getting off at the next stop, the observer might have pursued a different question, namely, whether the idioscene taking place in the car was ever replicated by the "same" idioclone. At the next station he would note that a new idioclone was formed as the result of people moving in and out the doors—a coming and going that continues until the end of the line, when the car is cleared of passengers and the idioscene terminates. The observer might then take up a vigil in the car to await the regrouping of the original idioclone. On successive days of riding back and forth, he might glimpse one or two of the idioclone members, but before long he would find out that the groups in the car are randomly assorted. Inspection of other cars on successive days would also fail to turn up the original idioclone, and the observer could reasonably conclude that the idioclone in question was a totally ephemeral entity.

In a Brazilian fishing village the repetition of multi-actor scenes produces a different kind of group. In the morning four men walk to the beach, put down their gear-boxes in a boat, the *Meu Xodo,* pull up sails, and set out to fish. Return inspection of the multi-actor scene locus (the boat *Meu Xodo*) reveals that not only is the fishing scene replicated on many different mornings, but that the initially observed idioclone, consisting of the "same" four men, is frequently reconstituted. The crew of the *Meu Xodo* is thus clearly differentiable from the type of group which assembles every evening in the subway car. (In formal terms, an idioclone which reconstitutes to perform a second instance of a given multi-actor scene will be called a *nomoclone*.)

At the end of a fishing idioscene, the members of the crew nomoclone leave the beach and separately enter into a variety of mono- and multi-actor scenes. The nomoclone in the boat never reconstitutes outside of the boat except in the presence of other actors. The crew of the *Meu Xodo*, in other words, meets only for performances of a series of idioscenes of the "same" scene. There are other nomoclones, however, which reconstitute in repeated idioscenes of a number of different multi-actor scenes. The group in the household kitchen, for example, usually meets for dinner as well as breakfast. It reconstitutes in the family car, in the backyard, in the living room, and its members frequently constitute the sole actors in the scene. However, it also reassembles in many other places where other actors are present.

In identifying nomoclones, it is important to insist that in at least one of the multi-actor scenes in which the clonic personnel participate, no other actors be present. Actors who frequently associate with each other, but always in the presence of additional actors, cannot be regarded as constituting a separate nomoclone. This does not mean that a nomoclone performs only in situations where no other actors are present. Indeed, as previously suggested, a nomoclone frequently associates with other nomoclones, with idioclones, and with random assortments of isolated individuals.

To explain the relationship between idioscenes, scenes, idioclones, nomoclones, and paragroups, consider a hypothetical population consisting of individuals *a*, *b*, *c*, *d*, *e*, *f*, *g*, . . . If *a*, *b*, *c* perform in idioscene *s*, then *a*, *b*, *c* constitute idioclone *I*:

IDIOSCENE	INDIVIDUALS	IDIOCLONE
s	*abc*	*I*

For nomothetic translation we inquire if idioclone *I* ever repeats idioscene *s*. If this occurs, then we speak of nomoclone *M* which performs in idioscenes *s*, *s*1, *s*2, etc.:

IDIOSCENE	INDIVIDUALS	NOMOCLONE *M* IDIOCLONE
s	*abc*	*I*
*s*1	*abc*	*I*
*s*2	*abc*	*I*

We now inquire if idioscenes *s*, *s*1, *s*2, etc. are ever repeated by a second set of actors. If *d*, *e*, *f*, *g* repeat *s*, then we may speak of scene *S* and idioclone *II*:

	IDIO-SCENE	INDI-VIDUALS	NOMO-CLONE *M*	IDIO-SCENE	INDI-VIDUALS	IDIO-CLONE
	s	*abc*	*I*	*s*4	*defg*	*II*
Scene	*s*1	*abc*	*I*			
S	*s*2	*abc*	*I*			
	*s*3	*abc*	*I*			

Repeated performance of *S* by idioclone *II* establishes nomoclone *N*:

	IDIO-SCENE	INDI-VIDUALS	NOMO-CLONE *M*	IDIO-SCENE	INDI-VIDUALS	NOMO-CLONE *N* IDIO-CLONE
	s	*abc*	*I*	*s*4	*defg*	*II*
Scene	*s*1	*abc*	*I*	*s*5	*defg*	*II*
S	*s*2	*abc*	*I*	*s*6	*defg*	*II*
	*s*3	*abc*	*I*	*s*7	*defg*	*II*

We may now also speak of a paragroup *P* defined by participation in *S; abcdefg* are seven members of *P* paragroup. Any other individuals who participate in *S* are also members of *P*. Suppose now that nomoclones *M* and *N* are found to reconstitute in several idioscenes of a second scene, *SQ*:

			NOMO-CLONE *M*			NOMO-CLONE *N*
Scene *S*	*s*	*abc*	*I*	*s4*	*defg*	*II*
	s1	*abc*	*I*	*s5*	*defg*	*II*
	s2	*abc*	*I*	*s6*	*defg*	*II*
Scene *SQ*	*sq*	*abc*	*I*	*sq4*	*defg*	*II*
	sq1	*abc*	*I*	*sq5*	*defg*	*II*
	sq2	*abc*	*I*	*sq6*	*defg*	*II*

On the basis of this small sample, it would be reasonable to hypothesize that other members of paragroup *P*, whom we have yet to identify, probably also perform in scene *SQ* as well as scene *S*.

Nomoclonic Types

In the preceding paradigm, nomoclones *M* and *N* may be spoken of as being representative of a particular *nomoclonic type,* defined by *M*'s and *N*'s separate participation in scenes *S* and *SQ*. Nomoclonic types, like paragroups, have an indefinite number of class members. They differ from paragroups, however, in being a class of groups rather than a class of actors. All the people in nomoclones *M* and *N* belong to the paragroup defined by scenes *S* and *SQ*. But the actors in nomoclones *M* and *N* cannot be spoken of as belonging to the associated nomoclonic type. They merely belong to nomoclones *M* and *N* which, in turn, are examples of a particular nomoclonic type.

As a limiting case, a nomoclonic type may be represented within a given population by only one extant nomoclone—for example, the ruling clique of a stratified society, such as the royal Hawaiian family. But with the passage of time, at least one additional member of the type must be observed, since the idioscenes which define the nomoclone's existence must rise to nomothetic status through replication by at least a second set of actors. Nomoclonic types, therefore, consist of two or more nomoclones, each of which may exist at the "same" or different moments in time.

Nothing prevents us from amplifying the diagnostics of a nomoclonic type by appealing to additional behavioral and biophysical features of the representative nomoclones. Suppose for example that *S* and *SQ* designate breakfast and dinner scenes respectively. We may now add *SR*, living room scene, as a further diagnostic of the household nomoclonic type. Following the lead of traditional ethnography, we may also choose to supply biophysical criteria. Thus we note that nomoclone *M* contains one adult male, an adult female, and one child; while nomoclone *N* contains an adult male, an adult female, and two children. The criteria by which we might now judge whether a third nomoclone, *O*, is representative of the same nomoclonic type as *M* and *N*, would consist of: performance of scenes *S*, *SQ*, *SR*; one adult male, one adult female, and one or more children. If we went further to discover that the adults were the biological parents of the children, we should be coming close to an operationalized version of the concept of nuclear or biological family.

Any nomoclone may be subjected to a similar sex, age, and genealogical analysis. The inventory of nomoclonic types possessed by a given population may thus be classified into nomoclones whose members are genealogically related, genealogically unrelated, or genealogically related in a particular way. (For example, all of the members of the nomoclones of a particular nomoclonic type may have a demonstrable male ancestor in common.) Or the nomoclones may be composed exclusively of males, or of females, or of children. In this fashion the nomoclonic repertories of different populations can be described with the intent of exposing interpopulation regularities. Needless to say, the statement of the conditions under which certain nomoclonic types can be expected to flourish, or give way to other nomoclonic types, is of paramount concern to cultural anthropology.

Primary Nomoclonic Types

In any population we may expect to encounter nomoclonic types which differ in the following important respects:

Size of Nomoclones: A nomoclone may contain as few as two (a married pair) or as many as a thousand (a freshman class) members.

Number of Nomoclones: There may be only one nomoclone of a particular type per generation (a royal family) or thousands of representatives (nuclear families).

Participation Ratio: Every member of the population may be a member of one of the nomoclones of a particular type (nuclear family), or only a small portion of the population may be involved (Plains Indian military societies).

Frequency of Idioscenes: The nomoclonic personnel may assemble only once or twice a year (a board of directors), or meet every day (husband and wife).

Variety of Scenes: The nomoclone may reconstitute for only one scene (fishing-boat crew), or for many different scenes (a boy-scout troop).

Nomoclonic Life-span: A nomoclone may endure for only several days (passengers on a ship), or for many years (partners in a business enterprise). It is important to bear in mind that the life of a nomoclone is equal to the time span during which the "same" set of actors perform in the nomoclone-defining scenes. Every performance of the diagnostic scene(s) by the total membership, without any additions or subtractions, is counted as part of the nomoclonic lifespan.

On the basis of these criteria, it is possible to state which nomoclones deserve ethnographic priority. Initial emphasis ought to be given to the identification of those nomoclones which embrace a high percentage of the population, reconstitute frequently, perform in many different multi-actor scenes, contain several actors per nomoclone, and have a long life-span. Such nomoclones may be considered as representative of *primary nomoclonic types*.

An inventory of primary nomoclonic types greatly facilitates the analysis of complex, multi-actor scenes, since actor-types may be supplied by reference to the actors' nomoclonic affiliations. Such an inventory permits the observer to approach a great variety of multi-actor scenes from a consistent point of view. Complex multi-actor scenes may thus be treated both as a source of additional nomoclonic constructions and as events involving a certain number of previously identified primary nomoclonic types.

In many populations, for example, the nomoclonic type, "household" (or "family"), is a convenient point of departure for cultural analysis. Almost every actor in the population can be assigned to one or another of the nomoclones in this nomoclonic type; each nomoclone contains several members, each of whom performs many different idioscenes per day, adding up to a total of many different scenes per year. New members are added usually no faster than one a year, with long periods when the membership is completely stable.

Permaclones

With the passage of time, a nomoclonic type is represented by nomoclones which bear a distinctive relationship to the earlier representatives of the type. New nomoclones sometimes contain certain members of old nomoclones who constitute, in a metaphorical sense, a kind of membership core. Consider, for example, the changes in the crew of the *Meu Xodo*. The nomoclone when first observed consisted of four individuals, *A*, *B*, *C*, and *D*. After three days of fishing, a fifth man, *E*, joined the others in performing the diagnostic idioscene. Two days later, *E* went back to fishing in another boat. Later, *D* became sick, and *A*, *B*, and *C* went out with a new man, *F*. Still later, the original four men were observed back in the boat. Hence, in a short while the *Meu Xodo* was the place coordinate in which three different nomoclones carried out fishing idioscenes:

Individuals	*Nomoclones*
ABCD	*M*
ABCDE	*M1*
ABCF	*M2*
ABCD	*M*

On the basis of the overlap in personnel, it is possible to group these successive nomoclones into an abstract structure whose life-span exceeds that of any of its constituent entities. Any time-ordered series of nomoclones of a given nomoclonic type which exhibit a similar overlap of personnel will be called a *permaclone*.

Many different kinds of membership overlap patterns may serve for the construction of permaclones. In the case of fishing-boat crews, short-run changes will in the long run give way to permanent changes having the following pattern:

ABCD
BCDE
CDEF
DEFG
EFGH

In this fashion all the original members of the original nomoclone will cease after a number of years to be members of the permaclone to which they belonged, yet the permaclone will continue to exist.

As long as the departing members of a nomoclone cease to appear in the scenes upon which the nomoclonic type is based, abrupt changes involving a large portion of the nomoclonic actors pose no special problem for identifying the permaclone. Even if our pattern of membership change involved the permanence of only one of the total personnel, the permaclonic affiliation would be easy to trace:

ABCDE
EFGHI
JKLME
ENOPQ

But if the actors formerly found together in a particular nomoclone regroup with other actors to form two new nomoclones of the same nomoclonic type, the permaclonic identity of the new nomoclonic associations may be hard to unravel. Consider, for example, nomoclones *M* and *N* consisting respectively of actors 1, 2, 3, 4 and 5, 6, 7, 8 of fishing-crew permaclones, *Meu Xodo* and *Estrela*. Suppose that as a result of an argument two crewmen of the *Meu Xodo* exchange places with two crewmen of the *Estrela,* forming nomoclones [1, 2, 5, 6] and [3, 4, 7, 8]. Under these circumstances, the criteria of personnel overlap will obviously be insufficient to decide with which of the permaclones each of the nomoclones ought to be identified. This dilemma might be resolved by considering the idioplace and idio-actone objects which are associated with the idioclones of a given permaclone. Actors 1, 2, 5, 6 could be considered the continuation of the *Meu Xodo* crew, since they are the ones who fish in the *Meu Xodo.* But this solution mirrors the vernacular confusion between place objects and groups. From the viewpoint of operational analysis, it would be more accurate to say that the life of the crew of both the *Meu Xodo* and *Estrela* had come to an end and that two new permaclones had been born.

Groups and Common Sense

The distinction between a nomoclone and the permaclone of which it is representative, is absent in most if not all vernacular systems of "ethnosemantics" (see p. 160). In the vernacular and even in the social sciences, groups roughly equivalent to nomoclones are spoken of as having a life-span independent of the lives of the constituent actors. Entities like the Kangaroo sib, the Mbundu patriline, and the New York Yankees are believed to maintain their nomoclonic identity no matter how many Kangaroos, Mbundus, or Yankees die, get born, quit, or join. This is not to say that people ordinarily confuse Joe Kangaroo with Harry Kangaroo, or Mickey Mantle Yankee with Joe DiMaggio Yankee. The ardent Yankee fan is quite aware that not a single member of the Yankees' 1910 team is playing ball for the Yankees today. Yet what it is precisely that links the 1961 team with the 1910 team is shrouded in the mystique of being a fan. To the grandstands, the Yankees are simultaneously a particular evanescent aggregate of specific individuals *and* a supra-individual entity, whose existence remains unaltered by the ceaseless comings and goings of specific players. There is, in effect, only one term for denoting the idioclones in the Yankee nomoclones, the nomoclones in the Yankee permaclone, and the Yankee permaclone itself. It thus becomes part of the ontological essence of the Yankees to be both personal and impersonal, mortal and immortal.

Certain common ideological devices may be better understood if we bear in mind the difficult chain of reasoning which is necessary for clearly distinguishing among idioclone, nomoclone, and permaclone. When confronted with the problem of describing the relationship between the evanescent, personal aggregates and the supra-individual, immortal groups, primitive ethnosemantic systems typically propound a variety of mystical dogma. The most widespread and probably the oldest of these mystical constructs is the principle of descent. By this principle, real or stipulated (undemonstrated) ancestors are classed together with their descendants to form supra-individual immortal groups. Successive idioclones, nomoclones, and even paragroups are typically linked together by the fiction of sharing "blood," milk, spirit-child incubi, ancestral souls, etc. These ideological devices vulgarly link Jews in the United States with Jews in Europe, Kangaroos with Kangaroos in

Australia, Sudras with Sudras in India, Royal Inca with Royal Inca in Peru, Africans with Africans in South Africa, and the Harry Joneses who have two children with the Harry Joneses who have five.

Vernacular constructions provide more semantic confusion by rarely, if ever, distinguishing between endogroups and paragroups. It is quite common, for example, to class together all the living members of a sib by virtue of their real or stipulated common descent regardless of whether those individuals included in the descent category ever jointly perform in any multi-actor scene. Since social scientists frequently base their own taxonomies of groups upon the ethnosemantic system in vogue among the people they are studying, it is often impossible to decide whether the existence of a given descent rule implies the existence of a nomoclone, permaclone, or simply a paragroup. Too frequently, all we really get to know is that the people believe that such and such a group exists, and that some believe they are members. I must vigorously protest the implication that the actor's belief is sufficient to call a nomoclone or permaclone into being. A belief held by an exclusive group of actors is a bit of shared verbal behavior which might entitle us to construct a paragroup. Endogroups, however, either have nonverbal actonic specialties in the form of exclusive participation in multi-actor scenes, or they do not exist.

True, the common fictions of descent may sometimes be interpreted as providing the psychological conditions under which a nomoclonic core is willing to accept newcomers and under which the newcomers are willing to "join." The children of the Harry Joneses, taught to believe that all children of their mother and father are equally members of the same family, are preconditioned to acting together in certain family nomoclone-defining scenes. But the mere belief that such a thing as a Jones "family" exists is insufficient to establish the existence of that entity. The Tembe patrisib of the Bathonga of Mozambique consists of people who believe they share common descent from a founding ancestor. Yet all the living Tembe never meet in any joint multi-actor scene. Hence, they are not a nomoclone and there can be no Tembe permaclone. The Jews in the United States believe that all descendants of Jews are Jews. Yet they too never meet in any joint multi-actor scene. Like the Tembe, they are simply a paragroup, defined by their distinctive repertory of verbal and nonverbal behavior units, among which there is always present the statement, "I am a Jew," or "I am a Tembe."

The vernacular failure to distinguish between nomoclones, permaclones, and paragroups probably arises from a universal tendency to assume the ultimate destiny of a group to be the achievement of permaclonic status. This is not to deny a general awareness of the fact that the actors of a given endogroup frequently cease to engage in their nomoclone-defining scenes at the first entrance of a new member or the first exit of an old. There are many subjectively recognized examples of short-lived nomoclones which do not rise to permaclonic status, as in the case of a nuclear family broken by divorce or the collapse of a business partnership. In these cases there is an everybody or nobody relationship between endogroup and scene. Yet many endogroups of the same nomoclonic types do rise to permaclonic status, and it is certainly the prevailing ideological plan that they should. There seems to be a widespread belief, in other words, that whatever is worth having nomoclonically, is worth having permaclonically. Indeed, I find it difficult to think of a *primary nomoclonic type, most* of whose constituent nomoclones do not rise to permaclonic status. It would appear to be a universal characteristic of human social organization that nomoclonic personnel are predisposed by verbal and nonverbal conditioning to continue their scenic specialties despite changes in group membership. In evolutionary perspective, this tendency is probably rooted in adaptive advantages associated with having endogroups which do not disappear at the first change in personnel. Indeed, the supreme triumph of human permaclonic organization is its ability to confer upon the population the continuance of complex, interactional, life-sustaining, multi-actor scenes, despite the eventual death of every member of every nomoclone.

Permaclonic Types

A *permaclonic type* is a class of permaclones, each of whose permaclones consists of nomoclones of the same nomoclonic type. In a given population, a permaclonic type may consist of a single permaclone, as *the* council of elders, or it may consist of a large number of permaclones, such as nuclear families or fishing crews. As previously suggested, most primary nomoclonic types are probably associated with permaclones. Hence, each primary nomoclonic type can be assumed to have its equivalent *primary permaclonic type*. But the criteria for distinguishing primary permaclonic types cannot be defined in precisely the same fashion as the criteria for primary nomoclonic types. As in the case of nomoclones, ethnographic attention is attracted by those permaclones to the nomoclones of which most of the population belongs, which consist of frequently reconstituted nomoclones, and which perform in many different kinds of scenes. But of special interest are the criteria of size and life-span. Permaclonic size and life-span are related in a fashion not possible among nomoclones.

The longer the life-span of a permaclone, the larger the number of people who have necessarily been members of the constituent nomoclones, despite the fact that the size of each of the constituent nomoclones may have remained stationary or actually grown smaller. A nomoclone can have a life-span no greater than that of its shortest-lived member, but a permaclone may theoretically endure as long as there are people on earth. Permaclonic life-spans may thus differ over a much wider range than is possible for nomoclones. Certain permaclones of the permaclonic type patrilocal band, for example, have endured for as much as twenty thousand years, while other permaclones, such as certain abortive criminal gangs, have had a life-span of only a few days or months. Those conspicuously durable permaclones, which transcend the lives of many generations of actors, have traditionally been of paramount interest to cultural anthropology. This interest is perfectly legitimate provided that it is not rationalized by claiming that the long-lived permaclones are somehow more strictly a part of the social structure, social organization, or culture, than the short-lived permaclones. The fact that the permaclones of a particular permaclonic type are characteristically short-lived does not necessarily mean that the permaclonic type itself is short-lived or confined to a single population. Hold-up gangs and military juntas, for example, are relatively short-lived permaclones, whose permaclonic type appears to be quite ancient.

Permaclonic Systems and Supersystems

Once a number of permaclones have been defined by specifying the multi-actor idioscenes in which the members of the constituent nomoclones constitute the exclusive cast of characters, further descriptions of the permaclonic entity may involve reference to mono- and multi-actor scenes and serials in which only some of the nomoclonic members participate, and in which members of other nomoclones, or random assortments of individuals, may also be found. In other words, given an inventory of nomoclones and nomoclonic types, permaclones and permaclonic types, further mono- and multi-actor scenes and serials may be described by specifying the actor-types in terms of the clonic affiliation of the participating actors. What results in either case is a description of the interrelationships which exist among the clonic entities.

Permaclonic and nomoclonic interrelationships may

take several different forms, depending upon the particular characteristics of the constituent relationship-defining scenes and serials. Some of the more obvious types may be listed as follows:

1. *Joint total participation in idioscenes:* All the members of nomoclones *M* and *N* participate jointly in instances of one or more multi-actor scenes.

> Example: The Joneses and the Smiths have dinner together several times a year.

2. *Joint partial participation in idioscenes:* Some members of nomoclones *M* and *N* participate jointly in repeated instances of one or more multi-actor scenes.

> Example: The Jones and Smith children ride to school together in the same car five times a week.

3. *Separate total participation in different scenes of the "same" serial:* All the members of nomoclone *M* participate in scene *SQ* of serial *R,* while all the members of nomoclone *N* participate in scene *SR* of serial *R.*

> Example: Every week 100 knife blades are made in Jose's blacksmith shop, picked up by Pedro, and carried to Antonio's brass-smith shop where handles are put on them.

4. *Joint partial participation in different scenes of the "same" serial:* Some members of nomoclone *M* participate in scene *SQ* of serial *R,* together with some members of nomoclone *N,* while some members of nomoclone *M* participate in scene *SR* of serial *R,* together with some members of nomoclone N.

> Example: The women from Misam's household and the women from Soma's household plant taro together in the cleared fields.

Any set of nomoclones related in one or more of the above ways will be said to constitute a nomoclonic system.

Insofar as the Joneses, the Smiths, Jose's shop, Antonio's shop, Misam's household, and Soma's household constitute instances of so many permaclones, and insofar as the successive nomoclones in these permaclones respectively preserve the indicated relationships, the permaclones in question may be said to form a permaclonic system.

Clonic interrelationships may also be expressed in terms of the nomoclonic and permaclonic types involved. Suppose that the population contains many household permaclones in addition to Soma's and Misam's, and that like Soma's and Misam's, certain pairs or triplets of these households are observed to clear and plant fields together. The ethnographer is now at liberty to report: "In this population separate households frequently clear and plant their fields together, the men from the households clearing and the women planting." Or suppose there are several blacksmith shops, and that in each case the brass-smiths put handles on blades made by the blacksmiths. The permaclonic system may now be described as: "In this population, the brass-smiths generally put handles on blades made by the blacksmiths." With this kind of statement, we have arrived at a level of abstraction approximately equal to that which is characteristic of standard ethnographic practice.

Finally, when a large number of scenically-specialized permaclones exhibit interrelationships through a large number of complex serials, we may speak of the existence of *permaclonic supersystems*. General Motors, the Pentagon, the Catholic Church, Columbia University, all are permaclonic supersystems made up of hundreds of separate permaclones, related to each other by a vast variety of different kinds of serials. On a still higher level of abstraction, these structures may be viewed as so many instances of types of permaclonic supersystems: American Manufacturing Corporations, Government Departments, Universities. Finally, they may be shown to exhibit interdependencies of their own, leading eventually to the specification of total socio-cultural systems.

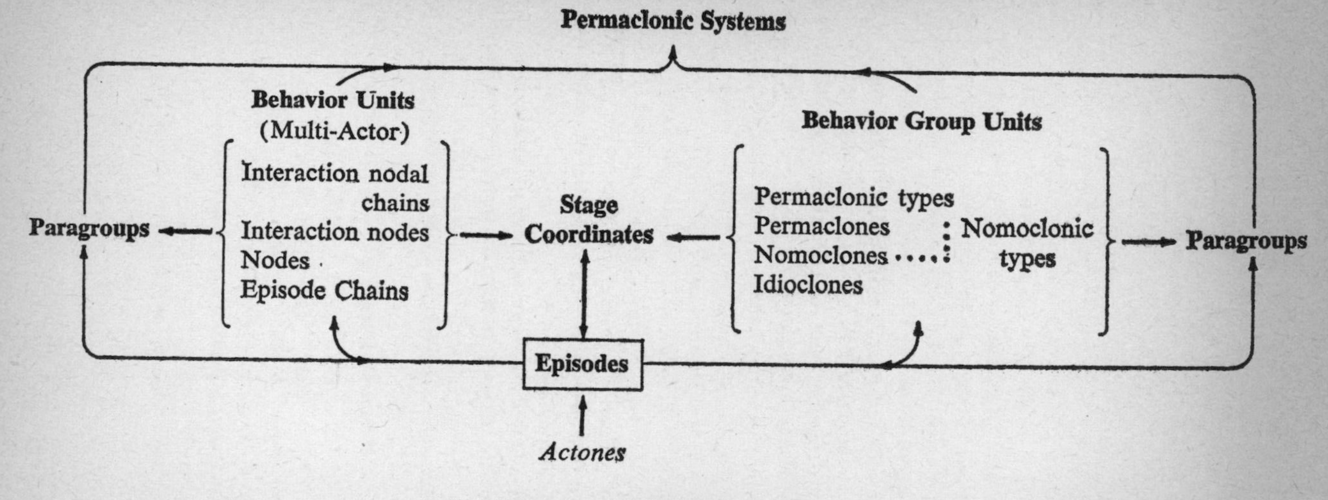
Permaclonic Systems
Behavior Units
(Multi-Actor)
Interaction nodal chains
Interaction nodes
Nodes
Episode Chains
Paragroups
Stage Coordinates
Behavior Group Units
Permaclonic types
Permaclones
Nomoclones
Idioclones
Nomoclonic types
Paragroups
Episodes
Actones
BEHAVIOR STREAM

Summary

The accompanying diagram sums up the ground which has been covered thus far. Note that all of the units refer to nonverbal behavior. Arrows trace the sources of diagnostics relevant for the construction of the respective units. The salient feature of the system is that episodes must be used for the construction of both higher-order behavior units and all indicated group units. Since an episode involves the specification of actor-type, and since group affiliation is a source of actor-type criteria, the analyst may move freely from group to behavior unit or from behavior unit to group once the system has been primed. This relationship is not completely symmetrical because behavior units need not always be based upon episodes whose actor-types are derived from group units, while all of the group units listed must refer, by definition, to episodic events. The asymmetry arises from the fact that provision must be made for priming the system, an operation involving reference to groups (and hence, actor-types) defined by biophysical rather than behavior features. No attempt has been made to elaborate a taxonomy of biophysical groups, for I believe such groups to be of little interest to the social science. However, the diagram indicates the possibility of using biophysical considerations for the qualification of behavior units and behavior group units, as well as for priming the system.

The extent to which the various entities may be compared from the point of view of level of abstraction requires further clarification. Up to a certain point the hierarchy is quite clear: the behavior stream is the lowest level; actones are a class of behavior stream events and episodes are in part a class of actones; episode chains are classes of episodes, nodes are classes of things extracted from episode chains, and nodal chains are classes of nodes. Scenes, however, need not necessarily be defined by reference to nodal chains, nodes, and episode chains (as when only a single episode is employed). The optional position of scenes in the meta-taxonomy hierarchy also places idioclones in an ambiguous position. If the multi-actor scene used to define an idioclone is based on an interaction nodal chain, the idioclone in question will then enjoy a logico-empirical status more abstract than that of an episode chain. But if the idioclone-defining behavior is merely a single episode, then idioclone and episode chain would be on approximately the same level of abstraction. Once this level is set, however, the hierarchy of behavior group units follows in ascending order of abstraction from idioclones to nomoclones to permaclones to permaclonic types. Under all options, permaclonic systems are the most abstract of the units.

If the option of complete, step-by-step abstraction is taken, it is theoretically possible that the description of a permaclonic system would involve at least nine distinctive operations repeated twice—assuming that the nomothetic status of the units is not in question: (1) episode, (2) episode chain, (3) interaction node, (4) interaction nodal chain, (5) multi-actor scene, (6) idioclone, (7) nomoclone, (8) permaclone, and (9) permaclonic type. Such ethnographic statements as "neighbors clear their fields jointly" or "patrilocal residence is practiced," despite their apparent simplicity, actually might be found to depend upon eighteen different operations, when subject to a strict, intersubjective, logico-empirical analysis. There would appear to be ample justification therefore for regarding ethnography as one of the most intricate and complex of human endeavors. That it does not always appear that way to most ethnographers stems from the fact that ethnography is dominated by an actor-oriented point of view. It seems simple because it is the actors who have performed the labor of abstraction—not individually, but collectively, during untold millennia of cultural evolution.

8

Emics and Etics

As we have seen, many fundamental behavior stream events can be classified into systematically related types of significant descriptive units without appeal to verbal happenings of any sort. My intention has not been to ignore verbal events, nor to minimize their evolutionary and functional importance. Rather, the strategy rests on the plain conviction that no systematic data language is possible where a mixture of verbal and nonverbal responses is the starting point for unit construction. This position is *not* opposed to the well-established hypothesis that the enormous repertory of nomothetic behavior characteristic of human populations owes its existence in large measure to the evolution of natural language. Indeed, the strategy in question is a logical consequence of those very features of human language generally regarded as being most distinctive, relative to infrahuman communication systems.

Verbal Behavior and Stage Coordinates

The grand achievement of natural language is the ability it confers upon the actor to learn responses which are biopsychologically appropriate to one set of stage coordinates while he is surrounded by a totally different set of stage coordinates. I have never seen a black widow spider, but I nonetheless already know what kind of response I should emit if I chanced to meet one crawling on my pillow. Sitting in my living room, I can tell a would-be traveler how to avoid a washed-out bridge on a road he has never seen in a country where he has not yet gone. Two housewives riding in a suburban bus exchange recipes for fancy desserts. This time-binding, place-binding capacity of language probably accounts in large measure for the prodigious size of the episodic repertory possessed by human populations. Through verbal reinforcement, responses acquired by one individual can be and often are duplicated by other individuals despite pervasive differences in their learning situations. Self- or other-administered verbal instructions normally accompany all types of human learning and greatly accelerate the rate of adding new responses to the individual's repertory.

The detachment or freedom from stage-setting which is so fundamental to the adaptive success of human communication systems is related to the employment of conspicuously unimportant or temporarily disposable body parts for the production of the primary signals in the system. The whole vocal complex, when not in use for chewing and swallowing, can be devoted almost entirely to the production of sounds which do not interfere with the manipulation of the environment by the vital prehensile and locomotive appendages of the body. To speak, one merely needs air, the most abundant of free goods.

Yet, because speech is largely independent of the specific environment in which an individual finds himself, it is, episodically speaking, the least regular of human responses. Despite the rigid patterning of the phonemic and morphemic levels, most conversations tend to be unpredictable, both as to message and time and place. The foods which one thousand randomly-selected American families will ingest at the breakfast table fall into a rather narrow range. But not the conversation. A man may punctuate his cornflake munching with reference to any subject under the sun—about yesterday, today, or tomorrow; about friends, relatives, or enemies; about politicians, baseball, food, clothing, or hydrogen bombs.

To the observer, this freedom of speech poses a fateful classificatory choice. A particular idioscene which is ripe for nomothetic translation in all but verbal characteristics may either be included or omitted from the general class. Shall we regard as separate scenes family breakfasts in which cornflakes are mixed with ruminations about the stock market, as opposed to breakfasts in which the conversation centers around Junior's report card?

An affirmative answer would effectively terminate our attempt to develop a data language for nonverbal behavior. If verbal (or any other kind of) message is accorded classificatory priority, then not only will idioscenes which are episodically very similar be counted as different, but idioscenes which are totally devoid of resemblance will have to be regarded as members of the same class of events.

Verbal versus Nonverbal Things

Of course, one might deliberately choose to emphasize message events at the expense of other behavior stream events. Standard ethnographic practices lean in this direction. Among most anthropologists, in fact, verbal events have traditionally been accorded greater emphasis than nonverbal events. The reason for this is rather obvious: words (or at least phonemes) are easily observed and easily recorded. In part, the preoccupation of the Boasians with the recording of oral textual material is understandable simply as a case of following the path of least resistance. A Kwakiutl myth is a behavior stream event which is rather easily described in an intersubjectively valid manner. After all, even without a sophisticated phonetic alphabet, vernacular messages are easier to describe than the episodic content of a complex multi-actor scene. If an actor says, "Fishing is a gamble," most English-speaking observers may be counted on to report faithfully that the actor said, "Fishing is a gamble." The point here is simply that a very reliable data language for the recording of verbal events already exists and is constantly in use. Hence there is a natural tendency to lean on this data language for ethnographic description. Moreover, few obstacles hinder those who seek to record verbal events independently of the scenic contexts in which they occur. Jokes, myths, riddles, songs, spells, prayers, curses, maxims, ethical imperatives, recipes, kinship terminologies, and other forms of folk taxonomies can be elicited on demand at the ethnographer's beck and call.

By emphasizing nonverbal units in this book, I do not mean to deny the importance of verbal behavior, nor to suggest that the verbal and nonverbal are unrelated categories of phenomena. But I insist upon an initial sharp separation between the two in the interest of facilitating both verbal and nonverbal analysis.

A Contrary View

Kenneth Pike, the distinguished linguist, holds to a view exactly contrary to the one just stated. According to Pike, "there is needed a unified theory, a unified set of terms, and a unified methodology" for both verbal and nonverbal behavior. In his *Language in Relation to a Unified Theory of the Structure of Human Behavior,* a work representing more than a decade of research and thought, Pike has made considerable progress toward his announced goal. Unfortunately, the intellectual tutelage under which he has proceeded, as reflected in his basic premises, renders this stupendous labor of little value for a science which is concerned with the study of the conditions under which similar entities recur in different populations.

Pike's basic orientation is supplied by him in a quote from Edward Sapir (Pike, 1954:9):

> It is impossible to say what an individual is doing unless we have tacitly accepted the essentially arbitrary modes of interpretation that social tradition is constantly suggesting to us from the very moment of our birth. Let anyone who doubts this try the experiment of making a painstaking report of the actions of a group of natives engaged in some activity, say religious, to which he has not the cultural key. If he is a skillful writer, he may succeed in giving a picturesque account of what he sees and hears, or thinks he sees and hears, but the chance of his being able to give a relation of what happens, *in terms that would be acceptable to the natives themselves,* are practically nil. He will be guilty of all manner of distortion; his emphasis will be constantly askew. He will find interesting what the natives take for granted as a casual kind of behavior worthy of no particular comment, and he will utterly fail to observe the crucial turning points in the course of action that give formal significance to the whole *in the minds of those who do possess the key to its understanding.* (Sapir, 1949: 546–547. Italics are mine.)

Pike calls this actor-oriented, subjective approach to cultural events the "emic" standpoint; the approach which attempts to achieve intersubjectivity, regardless of whether the native's sense of fitness is violated, he identifies as the "etic" standpoint:

> In contrast to the etic approach an Emic one is in essence valid for only one language (or one culture) at a time . . . it is an attempt to *discover* and to describe the pattern of that particular language or culture in reference to the way in which the various elements of that culture are related to each other in

> the functioning of that particular pattern, rather than an attempt to describe them in reference to a generalized classification derived in advance of the study of that culture. (8)

> An etic analytical standpoint . . . might be called "external" or "alien," since for etic purposes the analyst stands "far enough away" from or "outside" of a particular culture to see its separate events, primarily in relation to their similarities and their differences, as compared to the events of other cultures, rather than in reference to the sequences of classes of events within that one particular culture. (10)

> Etic criteria . . . have the appearance of absolutes, within the range of sensitivity of the measuring instrument (or of the expertness of the analyst); emic criteria savor more of relativity, with the sameness of activity determined in reference to a particular system of activity. (11)

Although Pike pays lip service to the importance of etic units— ". . . even the specialist, coming from one culture to a sharply different one, has no other way to begin its analysis than by starting with a rough, tentative (and inaccurate) etic description of it" (p. 11)—his treatment of etics is clearly unjust. All of his labor goes into showing how the discovery of verbal emic units—the "uttereme"—and emic nonverbal units—the "behavioreme" —require parallel and interlocking operations. He makes no attempt to show how one would go about finding etic units for nonverbal behavior. Indeed, the whole question of nonverbal etic units is summarily dismissed with a brief reference to Murdock and Ford's *Outline of Cultural Materials* (p. 73), which presents a kind of meta-taxonomy of cultural parts derived from an elaboration of Wissler's "universal pattern." The latter is notorious for its lack of logico-empirical grounding, consisting as it does of no more than a series of customary, *ad hoc* rubrics, extracted from tables of content of popular ethnographies. Neither Wissler's nor Murdock's universal rubrics can stand up to even a casual inquiry into their epistemological foundations, and it would be uncharitable to suggest that they were ever intended to be more than rough-and-ready work tools.

Pike himself admits that all emic analysis must begin with etic description. He also proposes that once the emic units have been discovered, they can be "listed for comparative purposes with the similar emic units from other languages (and cultures) so studied" (p. 12). But what shall be the grounds of communication, what the standards of similarity and difference, if one can be certain neither to begin with nor in final statement of the etic content of the sought-after emic units? An emic description, in short, can be no better than the etic units in which it must unavoidably be expressed. Pike commits this extravagant dislocation of cart and horse because, as previously suggested, in linguistics there happens to exist a very fine data language for etic—i.e., phonetic events. Once a linguist has decided that the sound-train denoted by the word "man" is an "uttereme" (that is, a morpheme), he has no great difficulty in communicating this fact to his colleagues in a thoroughly intersubjective fashion. Using a phonetic transcription, he indicates plainly what classes of sounds are involved in the utterance, "man." Independent observers trained in phonetics will then be able to identify recurrent cases of this segment of the sound stream with a degree of consensus not inferior to that found among a group of chemists looking for traces of a particular element in their test tubes. Unfortunately, there is no equivalently precise basis for intersubjective discourse when it comes to reporting nonverbal behavior stream events.[1]

[1] It is no accident that the most painstaking study of a psychiatric interview ever carried out contains references to nothing but verbal behavior. (See Pittenger, Hockett, Danehy, 1960.)

Purpose

An approach which emphasizes the viewpoint that is "acceptable to the natives themselves," which stresses the importance of the "whole" which is "in the minds of those who . . . possess the key to its understanding," and which seeks to "set down events as seen by the people" might be supposed to consist essentially of a verbal dialogue between observer and actor. If one wants to know what is going on inside an actor's mind, the obvious thing to do is to get him to tell you what he is thinking. Oddly enough, despite brave talk about the importance of what the actor thinks and feels, very few "emicists" appear to be ready to trust the native's own account of his inner life.

The operations which Pike proposes for the identification of behavioremes is typical of this lack of confidence in the native's ability to know his own mind. The behavioreme is partially defined as "an emic segment or component of purposive human activity" (p. 57). It thus becomes vital for the emic analyst to be able to identify the purpose of an actor's behavior.

> In spite of the problems which are involved, it is absolutely essential, if one is to study behavior *as it actually functions,* that one assume that the analyst can detect the presence and to some degree the nature of meaning and purpose. (80)

Pike is perfectly aware of the general arguments (some of which I have outlined in Chapter 5) against relying upon the actor's description of his own purposes:

> If we were limited to verbal comments by informants, important though these may be, the margin of error would be wider than it actually is, since people sometimes deliberately give false impressions about their purposes and meanings, or their observations and analytical ability may be poor, or the range of varia-

tion of purpose within a body of participants may be so large as to leave verbal reports confused or conflicting. (78)

The obvious implication of these remarks is that since the actor himself is frequently not sure of his own purpose or meaning: (1) It is futile to suppose that the observer is going to be able to find out what that purpose or meaning really is; (2) It is possible that any given behavioral event may have as many subjective meanings and purposes as there are actors participating in them; (3) The purpose and meaning of any given actor may simultaneously include each and every purpose of all of the actors. The emicists, however, are indefatigable. Despite all the evidence to the contrary, and despite their inability to specify the operations, they continue to look for *the* "correct" or "central" purpose of a church service, family breakfast, football game, etc. Apparently, somewhere beyond the verbal confusion and analytic unreliability of the actor, lies a valley of inner subjective truth. The nature of this hidden land is further obscured by Pike's admission that not only can both the actor and the analyst be in error about the subjective purpose or meaning of a behavioral event, but the purpose and meaning may actually be "indeterminate in certain instances." Referring to the problem of deciding whether the element *port* has the same meaning in *porthole* as it does in *portal* and *porter*, Pike observes:

> The data may be such that there are partial phonetic and partial semantic resemblances between certain of these items, but the decision at some point must be arbitrary as to the assignment of some of the most perplexing of these items, since a theory of the structure of behavior must leave room for variants in both form and meaning, *but without being able to provide any absolute measure of just how much alike or just how different either form or meaning or the form-*

> *meaning composite may be before one can no longer equate two items.* (80. Italics are mine.)

Obviously, as I have taken pains to indicate in Chapter 1, *all* classificatory decisions are arbitrary in that they are man-made interruptions of continua. But an even greater misapprehension follows when Pike goes on to equate these arbitrary qualities of his classificatory principles with some supposed special innate indeterminacy of certain behavior stream phenomena:

> In our present theory we state that the indeterminacy lies in the data, within the structure, and that any arbitrary attempt to force a decision one way or another in certain instances does violence to the structure rather than clarifying it. (80)

Here Pike continues to present a basic condition of scientific knowledge as if it were unique to the study of certain behavior stream events. It is an inescapable consequence of the infinite potential of calibration that all classificatory ranges will be vague, ambiguous, or indeterminate at their extreme limits. But it is a fundamental condition of scientific inquiry that all such vagaries, ambiguities, and indeterminacies be reduced to the least possible number by constantly striving to increase the precision of our measuring apparata, and by striving to insure the replicability of all measuring operations. One cannot ask of an emic approach that it provide us with a totally unambiguous data language; such a language is not possible even in physics. But one can certainly demand that the data language display a sense of responsibility to the task of maximizing intersubjectivity. I do not believe that Pike's operations for discovering *the* "essential wholes" (p. 33) in nonverbal behavior can pass this test. Pike would have us believe, for example, that despite the variety of purposes, interests, meanings, and levels of attention characteristic of the actors in a church service, analysts may nonetheless uniformly arrive at a conception of the service as a whole which represents a common emic unit to the churchgoers themselves. In order to do this, he proposes that we disregard the motives of those actors who in Pike's judgment are not "actual participants" in the scene, even though they are there in church as plain as life:

> If . . . we assume that in order to demonstrate that a segment is emically a "whole" we need do so only in reference to persons acting as actual participants— *not in reference to critics, or pseudo-participants*— then a usable though not precise criterion can be found. (33. Italics are mine.)

This bit of emic sleight-of-hand clearly presupposes that one can distinguish the genuine actors from the spurious, just as Sapir, some time ago, proposed that one could distinguish genuine from spurious cultures (Sapir, 1949). If there are such things as pseudo actors, obviously we can find them only after finding the genuine ones. But Pike's only advice on how to find the genuine actors consists of assurances that they are the ones who are left over after the "ringers" have been identified.

Insofar as Pike himself admits that purposes and meanings frequently cannot be obtained from the observation of verbal behavior, and that, moreover, they often cannot be obtained at all, there is built into the emic approach an extraordinarily high tolerance for idiosyncratic intuitions. What starts as an attempt to find out what the native thinks, ends as an attempt to outguess him. Sometimes the native is wrong; sometimes he is right. Sometimes he is a good source of information; sometimes not. Sometimes he doesn't know what his purposes are but the observer does. Sometimes he knows but the observer doesn't. Sometimes neither of them knows and there is nothing anyone can do to find out. Pike's emic approach, when applied to nonverbal behavior, neither establishes what is going on in the mind of the native, nor guarantees to us that anything is going on at all, except in the mind of the observer.

The Emics of Barker and Wright

An independent but strikingly parallel emic approach to the problem of recording and analyzing verbal and nonverbal behavior stream events appears in the work of psychologists Roger Barker and Herbert Wright and their students. Their fundamental assumption is that it is both necessary and possible to record behavior as the actors experience it. As in Pike's approach, their basic analytical units—"episodes"—consist both of verbal and nonverbal behavior. And their final results are predictably inappropriate for the intersubjective identification of nomothetic cross-culturally valid units.

A brief account of Barker and Wright's work cannot do justice to the complexity of their data-collecting methods and the richness of their analytical procedures. *Midwest And Its Children* is in many ways the most painstaking, detailed, and brilliant analysis of human behavior that has ever been achieved. Yet all of this effort is based on premises which are transparently ill-suited to the task at hand.

The psychologist Kurt Lewin stands to Barker and Wright as Edward Sapir stands to Pike. Lewin's formula for the description of behavior includes a mandatory calculus of the individual's "life-space"—the totality of things within and outside the individual which at any moment are supposed to be psychologically important to him. This leads Barker and Wright to quote with approval Lewin's belief that

> The most complete and concrete descriptions of (behavior and) situations are those which writers such as Dostoevski have given us. These descriptions have attained . . . a picture that shows in a definite way

> how the different facts in an individual's environment are related to one another and to the individual himself. (Lewin, 1936:13, quoted in Barker and Wright, 1955:196)

Under Lewin's tutelage, Barker and Wright concentrate upon recording behavior so as to enable independent analysts to identify "molar" units. The latter are built up of "molecular" events consisting of behavior recorded under a relatively high magnification of small body-part motions. These molecular activities—elbow-bending, exterior adjustments of the fingers, perspiration, chewing, swallowing, grasping, movements of the lips, tongue, etc. —have a role to play in the behavior record, but they are not essential to the construction of higher-order molar "episodes." *Since the actor is not supposed to be aware of them, they are not considered to form part of his "life-space"; indeed, they aren't even considered part of the "whole person":*

> They necessarily engage only subordinate and more or less independent parts or mechanisms of the person. A child in going about his business as a whole person never perspires in running to school or salivates in buying candy; and a child rarely, if ever, bends his arms in saluting the flag or wags his tongue in reciting a lesson. He runs to school, buys the candy, salutes the flag, and recites the lesson while, contemporaneously, lesser systems do the sweating, salivating, bending, and wagging with greater or lesser independence of the person as a superordinate whole. (178–9)

In contrast, molar behavior "is goal directed; and it generally occurs within the cognitive field of the person" (p. 179).

The purposive nature of the episode is also referred to as its direction:

> The centermost criterion of an episode derives from a principal characteristic of molar behavior, directedness. It provides that the behavior from the beginning to the end of an episode is constant in direction. (236)

When the direction changes, a new episode begins. Concerned with establishing "the empirical manageability of direction as an attribute of molar behavior units" (p. 240), Barker and Wright propose seven objective "marks" by which this emic essential is to be identified. All seven resemble each other and Pike's nonverbal criteria of purpose in one obvious respect: each is an attempt to operationalize the emic essence through the substitution of one vague term for another, like a hot potato being tossed back and forth. For example, the first "mark" of direction is: "Action persists in the absence of instigating conditions." How one is to tell when instigating conditions are present or absent is not specified, except in what appears to be a kind of psychological free verse:

> The instigating conditions act more like a goal than a continuing push from behind. They set the action off; then, in a sense, the action maintains itself, not in a situational vacuum; yet without continuance of the initial stimulus factors. (238)

Mark 2 is:

> Change in position toward a part of the environment is renewed after forced digression or delay.

How one is to tell whether the change in position which followed the delay was the continuation of the movement which preceded the delay, is left unresolved. Mark 3 is:

> 'Preparatory adjustments' appropriate to imminent situational change, toward which the observed action contributes, accompany the action.

We are informed neither how to identify a preparatory adjustment, nor how to arrive at an adjustment appropriate to situational change. The remaining signposts of direction are all written in the same brand of jargon.

Like Kenneth Pike, Barker and Wright persist in their search for *the* essential direction or goal of the actor's behavior, even while admitting that the evidence of observed behavior must frequently be disregarded to find this essence:

> . . . the episoder has to recognize that direction is a genotypic factor in behavior which can be clothed in diverse phenotypes; there are no behavioral specifics for either constancy or change in this behavior factor. (243)

The impression that finding the direction of an episode is at bottom a matter of guesswork is further strengthened by a remark which seems to indicate that formal criteria of direction are really superfluous, since an actor's goal comes to the observer like a gestalt:

> In reality, however, the required judgments usually are not analytical. The direction of the behavior in relation to the new position and vice versa generally are immediately apprehended; the unity of action in an episode is perceived almost as immediately as the unity of a visual form or an auditory pattern. (240)

Of course it is admissible that a number of independent observers might be found to agree that certain sections of the behavior stream constitute unitary, goal-seeking performances. Indeed, insofar as observers drawn from a common population may be presumed to acquire similar "plans" (see below), they will tend to reach agreement on what has occurred, provided the episodes being watched are part of their common experience. But as I have previously suggested (pp. 24-25), such agreement evaporates when foreign behavior events are under consideration. Similar difficulties would undoubtedly arise were unacculturated foreigners included in the observer team. One cannot escape the conclusion that the extension of the emic viewpoint to nonverbal behavior is doomed to generate nothing but intuitive, culture-bound, and subjective descriptions.

Differences between Verbal and Nonverbal Behavior

The ultimate source of the emicist's difficulties lies in the attempt to impose upon nonverbal behavior the type of approach which has proved successful for verbal behavior, on the mistaken assumption that, since both verbal and nonverbal behavior are behavior, a single standpoint should be equally appropriate to both.[2] Certain linguists (Block and Traeger, 1942: Z. Harris, 1951) reject the notion that phonemes and morphemes can be isolated only by identifying the actor's "meaning," but as an outsider, I find little to resist in the emic standpoint when applied to verbal behavior. Here, an emic approach seems useful if not necessary for the identification of the message-carrying parts of verbal events. These events are instances of a complex communication system, and any communication system must ultimately be resolvable into compound units whose "key," "code," "purpose," or "meaning" is roughly agreed upon (consciously or unconsciously) by all users of the system. Indeed, the system derives its adaptive importance precisely from its ability to convey, at least some of the time, relatively unambiguous bits of information from one actor to another. Hence, the data language of linguistics quite rightly consists of units whose emic classificatory criteria are systematically checked against the informant's opinions about whether certain sounds are "important" or "mean the same thing."

In the case of language, the entire population of semantically intact, enculturated adults exhibits a highly

[2] A similar assumption is to be found in Gerard, Kluckhohn, and Rapoport, 1956.

refined sensitivity to minute variations in the components of utterances. Certain classes of sounds—the morphemes —must be present if a message is to be sent or received, and a very high level of agreement exists as to whether or not the criteria of membership in these sound classes has been fulfilled although considerable disagreement may obtain as to the actual referential "meaning" and "semantic equivalence" of the message itself.

The high level of sensitivity to deviations in sound production is the result of years of intensive training. As the child matures, reinforcement is withheld for all but the closest approximations to the parental and social standards, and every error is greeted with derision or some other sign of disapproval. The whole process of linguistic enculturation is aided by the fact that, although the child is faced with learning how to produce several thousand different words, all of these words are built up out of only a handful of emically significant sounds—the phonemes. In adding to his vocabulary, the child unconsciously and automatically limits his efforts to combining already familiar sounds in new and unfamiliar sequences. After a while, the speech community need correct only the sequence of phonemes, rather than the phonemes themselves, because the ability to produce "incorrect" or "deviant" sounds in message context has been thoroughly inhibited.

To propose an emic approach to nonverbal behavior is, in essence, to place upon the actors the burden for deciding whether or not two events are similar. This makes sense in the case of communication systems because the actors have spent their lives training to make such decisions and they are usually in substantial agreement. Moreover, there is only one way to communicate with people, namely, by acquiring similar standards of "identity" with respect to the components of their communication system. In the case of most nonverbal behavior, however, the community is relatively lax in the enforcement of its standards. It is easy to decide between the right and wrong way to pronounce 10,000 or so morphemes; it is another matter for a population to reach consensus on the right and wrong way to perform forty or fifty million episodes. Whether my family's breakfast is equivalent to Professor Pike's family's breakfast cannot be solved by asking the actors to vote on the issue. The community of observers themselves must decide this question. They alone can resolve it in the manner best serving the interest of theory-construction. To leave it up to the informants, is, in effect, to abandon social science to amateurs. On the other hand, if we want to know whether two vernacular messages are similar or different, there can be no higher authority than the actors themselves.

9

Verbal and Nonverbal Units

An ethnographer's interest in verbal behavior[1] lies, as in the case of nonverbal behavior, with the replicative or nomothetic aspect of utterances. Unique utterances, or unique combinations of utterances, are of no interest except as they may provide idiographic material for the construction of nomothetic classes. I shall not discuss here those classes of verbal events which are the subject matter of descriptive linguistics. Phonemes, morphemes, and grammatical rules are cultural entities about whose epistemological status a nonlinguist cannot hope to be enlightening. I shall instead be concerned with higher-level verbal entities which can be constructed, given a knowledge of grammar and lexicon.

From an etic point of view, the only criterion of whether or not two utterances are similar is the degree to which they are phonetically isomorphic. From this stand-

[1] By verbal behavior I mean all behavior events which are part of a communication system—speaking, gesturing, etc.

point, the verbal event, "^{3}hâw + ^{2}ówld + âhrya'" is replicated only by a second occurrence of "^{3}hâw + ^{2}ówld + âhrya'." Proceeding exclusively on this basis, an ethnographer would be able to identify chains of utterances, some of which would be associated with particular actor-types, scenes, or groups. Poems, plays, songs, proverbs, salutations, clichés, military and sports commands, oaths, prayers, advertisements—all tend to display a high degree of phonetic, phonemic, and morphemic isomorphism. But from an emic point of view, almost perfectly similar messages may be totally nonisomorphic. The utterance, "How old are you?" bears practically no resemblance to the utterance, "When were you born?" Yet, from an emic point of view, they are mutually substitutable under certain conditions. That is, some actors will say that the two utterances "mean the same thing."

Semantic Equivalence

This fact raises a most disturbing specter. If similar meanings are conveyed by etically different utterances, is it not also the case that different meanings are conveyed by etically similar utterances? For example, fishermen in a Brazilian village often express the opinion that "fishing is a matter of luck." The storekeeper, who has never gone to sea, also asserts that "fishing is a matter of luck." Yet he cannot know in the way a fisherman knows under what conditions skill, courage, and hard work can be overwhelmed by the vagaries of wind, current, and marine biota. Or consider the corporation executive who has been promoted to a higher position. His colleagues shake hands with him and say, "congratulations." For some, this message means, "I am happy for you. You deserve it." For others, "It should have been me." Deeper and deeper levels of emic significance await those who care to probe into the idiosyncratic context of a particular message. Finding out what people "really mean" is a daily, unending concern shared by all human beings, in courtship, play, or business.

There are, then, essentially three options which may be followed in the task of establishing supragrammatical emic regularities:

1. All etically similar utterances are semantically equivalent, but no etically different utterances are equivalent, regardless of the subjective intentions of the actors.
2. Semantic equivalence in the case of etically similar or different utterances exists only when the total subjective inner states of the actors are congruent.
3. All etically similar utterances are equivalent, *and some* etically different utterances may be equivalent, the equivalence in the latter to be determined without appeal to the subjective, inner intentional state of the actors.

The first option carries the conviction that synonymy[2] does not exist. It seems to me, however, that a purely pragmatic type of synonymy can be demonstrated in all natural languages simply by substituting certain words and phrases in a given utterance and inquiring whether the meaning has changed. As long as the question of synonymy is posed with respect to *abstract* situations, we may expect *some degree* of concordance. Dictionary meanings are thus wholly conventional and abstract listings of mutually substitutable words and phrases. In the abstract many (*but not all*) speakers of English will agree that the phrase, "Fishing is a matter of luck," can be substituted (that is, be a semantic equivalent) for "Fishing depends on chance." Some may disagree, but if it is stressed that it is approximate and not absolute equivalence which is at stake, the concordance will normally be high. To be sure, the majority of speakers will not always agree on

[2] For a discussion of the vexed philosophical problem of synonymy and translatability, see Quine, 1960, and McGee, 1959.

each and every substitution. But to deny the possibility of synonymy in the above sense would seem to challenge the principle on which dictionaries are constructed. I conclude, therefore, that the first option is based on an unnecessarily rigid and altogether too narrow concept of meaning.

In the second option, the criterion of conventional abstract equivalence is abandoned to pursue what a given word or phrase means to particular actors at a particular time and place. One now asks whether Francisco, the fisherman, meant the same thing as Abilio, the storekeeper, when each said, "Fishing is a gamble." Does Francisco really believe that it is his luck and not his skill that is engaged? Does Abilio, who has never gone out in a boat, mean the same thing by "fishing" as Francisco does? This aspect of semantics the ethnographer had better leave to the novelist or the psychiatrist. It is their task, not his, to tell us what people *really* mean when they use particular words and phrases in given situations. But I believe they labor in a bottomless pit. Two readers often arrive at an entirely different subjective understanding of a given novel, both equally acceptable to the author; a patient may struggle for years to tell his psychiatrist what the word "mother" really means to him. If meaning in the first option is construed too narrowly, it is given an altogether vague and whimsical interpretation in the second.

This leaves us with the third option as the most reasonable criterion of semantic equivalency for *vernacular or natural languages*. This option admits the possibility of conventionalized synonymy, but rejects outright the possibility of establishing synonymy which includes individualized psychobiological nuances. It further implies the existence of a discoverable set of syntactic rules for combining terms by which one phrase may be substituted for another.

I shall make no attempt here to develop in detail the operations whereby semantic equivalency of the third type can be established for an extensive corpus of verbal behavior. Obviously, it is possible in every language to learn how to ask the equivalent of the question, "What does this utterance mean?" When the answer is in the form of another utterance, and is acceptable to a significant portion of the speech community, semantic equivalence has been established. Undoubtedly, many pitfalls must be overcome, as anyone can testify who has tried to translate a foreign language with a dictionary. But what we are after is neither the perfect synonymy of the logicians, nor the will-o'-the-wisp of the depth psychologists. All that is needed for the construction of certain kinds of emic regularities is a rough-and-ready approximation.

Verbal Analysis of Scenes: Subscenes

Despite the general unpredictability and irregularity of verbal behavior in relation to scenic context, some classes of idioscenes regularly contain some utterances which are semantically equivalent in the above sense. Appeal to these verbal regularities presents the opportunity of further refining the classification of a population's scenic repertory as part of a higher stage of ethnographic description.

Idioscenes which contain similar nodal chains can be classified into separate *subscenes*, in accordance with their verbal content. The term *subscene* is intended as a reminder that episodically similar idioscenes cannot be set apart from each other solely on the basis of verbal content. The strategy which has been followed up to now demands that verbal content enter as a scenic modifier only after the actonic comparisons have been completed.

If each of the idioscenes of a particular scene features a different set of verbal events, or verbal events whose similarity is no greater than one would expect to find in any random sample of utterances, then the verbal content of the scene is scarcely worth noting (except insofar as material is being gathered for an analysis of such units as ideology or themes). Any departure from what might be expected if verbal events were randomly distributed deserves to be recorded. For example, as multi-actor scenes usually contain some conversation, the absence of conversation, as in a crowded subway car, is a noteworthy ethnographic detail. Mono-actor scenes, on the other hand, are usually performed in silence. Hence, singing in a bathroom attracts attention.

Episodically, a college course on Chaucer bears close resemblance to a course on social stratification, but they can readily be distinguished as subscenes on the basis of verbal content analysis. Business and government office scenes also resemble each other in their episodic content, which centers around such actone objects as telephones, typewriters, file cabinets, pencils and pens, water coolers, etc. The differential nature of the commodities or services referred to in the oral and written communications would establish subscenes defining particular categories of business enterprises or government bureaus. Many denominational church scenes are probably episodically similar but verbally distinguishable. The luncheon conversation of a group of doctors probably follows paths not trod by a group of engineers or dress designers, but everybody in the restaurant will ingest his food with the aid of similar actone objects.

Note that instead of focusing upon the probable verbal content of scenes as a means of refining the classification of nonverbal behavior, one might reverse the emphasis and classify utterances in conformity with the kinds of scenes in which they are apt to occur. Both enterprises properly belong in the totally neglected field which Dell Hymes (n.d.) has called "ethnography of speaking." Obviously, no progress in this area can be made until an etic method for describing nonverbal behavior is developed which systematically separates verbal from nonverbal behavior.

Referential Meaning

In our foregoing discussion of the meaning of utterances, the question of just what aspects of the universe a particular word or phrase denotes was studiously avoided.

Consideration of this issue is irrelevant to the identification of subscenes by appeal to semantically equivalent verbal regularities. Referential meaning, as distinct from semantic equivalence, requires a separate type of ethnographic analysis designed to heighten our understanding of linguistic systems rather than of scenic regularities.

The rules of science demand an attitude of profound skepticism with respect to the ability of natural languages to achieve intersubjectivity. One cannot assume that semantic equivalency (isomorphic or nonisomorphic) carries with it uniformity of logico-empirical reference. Indeed, the only way to achieve such uniformity is by stating the logico-empirical operations which have been employed in the construction of designated classes of things. Lacking such operations, natural terms designate classes of phenomena which are not consistently or dependably intersubjective. Thus, it is a wholly empirical issue whether two speakers of a given natural language will designate a particular event (as operationally defined by the community of observers) by the same or semantically equivalent term, rather than by different or semantically nonequivalent terms.

Consider, for example, the classification of racial types in a Brazilian fishing village. The term "branco" is the semantic equivalent of "uma pessoa que tem cor branco e cabello bon," which in turn has the English semantic equivalent "a person who has white skin and soft, straight hair." About the Portuguese equivalency, "Branco" equals "Cor branco e cabello bon," there is almost universal agreement among the villagers (but I cannot vouch for the English translation). Yet when a sample of 100 villagers was asked to identify the racial type of a particular individual who appeared to the observers to satisfy the criteria of "branco," only 56 per cent called her "branca" while 16 per cent called her "morena clara," and 6 per cent called her "mulata clara," etc. In one case twelve different, nonequivalent terms were applied to a single subject (Harris and Kottak, 1963).

Very little is known as to how much lack of agreement about referential meaning exists in linguistic systems. Certainly some vacillation in the application of a natural term to an actual situation may be expected at the logico-empirical extremes of the class of phenomena designated by all natural words and phrases. Even operationally-validated artificial terms contain a certain amount of vagueness. English speakers probably approach universal agreement that the term "boy" is semantically equivalent to "a male younger than a man but older than an infant." Yet if we inquire whether a particular college junior is a man or a boy, conflicting opinions will surely arise. Bushes are lower than trees, but is this overgrown privet a small tree or a large bush? Housewife and grocer agree that a ripe tomato has a deep red color and yields to the touch, but this does not prevent them from arguing over the particular specimen in the scale. Life is full of minor and major clashes of opinion about referential meaning. Is the room hot or cold, the girl homely or striking, the mayor honest or conniving, the press free or controlled, the wife loving or neglectful? One picture is worth a thousand words for two quite different reasons: first, it takes a long time to verbally describe a complex scene; second, a picture has the supreme virtue of not requiring the observers to tell each other what they see. To put it another way, silence is golden because it provokes no disputes.

Despite the prevalence of referential vagueness, articulation between natural terms and empirical entities is not generally so hopelessly confused that vulgar communication leads to evolutionarily inadaptive responses as far as the total population is concerned. I for one would not be surprised if most people were found to disagree as much as they agree about referential meaning. But in certain adaptively critical areas of behavior, it must be assumed that natural languages possess a hard core of intersubjectivity. This hard core of referential consensus is made possible by the fact that, in its local habitat, a given population is not confronted with all the empirically extant grades and intergrades of physical, biological, and cultural phenomena.

Consider, for example, the use of language as an instrument of coordination among the crew of a fishing boat. The boat arrives over the fishing bank and the captain says, "Drop anchor." The crew responds without hesitation by picking up a heavy stone, around which are wrapped pointed sticks, and by letting this stone down over the side of the boat. They never respond to the captain's order by dropping the oar, the baitbasket, the mast, or the rudder over the side. There appears to be complete, infallible intersubjectivity with respect to the referential meaning of the term "anchor." But this intersubjectivity is illusory, for it is valid only for the particular scene in which it has been pragmatically tested and wherein the contrast between the anchor and every other part of the boat is of the most glaring sort. If the same crew were confronted with a graded series of heavy objects of different sizes, shapes, densities—some with pointed sticks, others with blunt ones, others with no sticks, some with ropes attached, others with heavy cables, some hollow, some cup-shaped, some with prongs, some smooth, etc.—and asked individually to pick out those which are anchors, the same kind of disagreement might be exhibited as when they were asked to identify who in their village was a "branco." Similarly, one ordinarily encounters what seems to be a high degree of intersubjectivity as to which objects in an American living room are chairs and tables. Yet certain intergrades could easily be constructed which would stimulate some informants to insist that they were tables and others to insist that they were chairs.

Although anthropologists have paid practically no attention to the problem of referential meaning *within* a given population (with the exception of color categories and kinship), they have long been familiar with the fact that the referential meanings of different linguistic systems are frequently incongruous or overlapping and imply the existence of different conscious or unconscious classificatory assumptions.[3] In some cases, entire fields of referential distinctions present in one language are absent in another: Tupi languages have many words for parrots; Eskimo specializes in distinguishing different varieties of snow; Brazilian Portuguese has forty different terms for racial types, etc. Elsewhere, referential meanings cross-cut each other in crazy-quilt fashion, as in contrasting kinship terminologies, and folk taxonomies of disease, plants, and animals. There is no reason, however, to suppose that similar differences do not also exist in the referential systems of individuals who share the "same" language.

Ethnosemantics

All human populations use their communication systems to describe the inorganic, organic, and super-organic phenomena present in their habitats. The classifications and rules of classification, explicit or implicit, by which equivalencies and/or referential meanings are generated, and all other verbal behavior which involves descriptive statements, constitutes an ethnographic subdiscipline which will be called here ethnosemantics.

Of special interest in this field are certain restricted, logically consistent, semantic subsystems which, upon analysis, can be reduced to a small set of formal semantic rules. The most successful attempts to formulate such rules have been restricted thus far to the domain of kinship terminologies (Goodenough, 1956; Wallace and Atkins, 1960; Lounsbury, 1956). Attention has also been directed to ethnobotany (Conklin, 1954) and to ethnoecology and ethnomedicine (Frake, 1962; 1961).

The rules in question fall into two types: (1) Rules for identifying occasions in which one of a set of verbal responses is appropriate for the actors; (2) Rules for identifying when one of a set of nonverbal responses is appropriate for the actors. In the first case, the analyst

[3] Benjamin Whorf (1956) has argued that these classificatory assumptions are responsible for differences in nonverbal behavior.

states when it is appropriate for any ego to call another person "uncle," "cousin," "brother," etc., or to call a particular combination of aches, swellings, and inflamations a "sore," a "boil," or a "wound," etc. In the second case, the analyst states, for example, when it is appropriate for a set of actors to decide to move their house sites or clear new fields (Frake, 1962). Both kinds of formal semantic rules, it will be noted, are equally unrelated to nonverbal behavior. To know that an uncle is a "first degree, collateral ascending generation male," is to say nothing about uncles as a paragroup, or nomoclone. To know that people say they will move their houses when they are too close to their neighbors, is to impart no information about when people actually do move to another house site. It is even doubtful that the formal semantic rules of either type really tell us when people will actually emit the verbal responses in question. All that the rules may express are the conditions which people *say* will be appropriate for them to say something—a folk-form of meta-language analysis. Frake admits this as being the case for his analysis of Subanum disease categories:

> It is difficult, then, to define Subanum diagnostic categories in terms of analytic or perceptual attributes of their denotata. . . . Since one cannot point to a disease entity and say "That's such and such" as one can with a plant specimen, and since no one individual ever personally experiences but a fraction of the total number of diseases he can, in fact, differentiate, the Subanum themselves must learn to diagnose diseases through verbal descriptions of their significant attributes. (1961:124)

In other words, the Subanum says that when he sees a sore he will call it (if asked) a *bedult*. But since we never get a chance to see the Subanum inspecting a sore, we never know whether he will in fact say it is a *bedult* when he sees one. Further, if he will indeed say *bedult* when he sees one, we never know what conditions are necessary to make him see one. This, of course, is merely another way of indicating the existence of referential vagueness as an unavoidable feature of all natural languages.

The epistemological status of componential analysis of kinship terminologies is somewhat more difficult to decipher. According to Frake the semantic rules of kinship synoptically describe the ". . . necessary and sufficient conditions by which an investigator can determine whether a newly encountered instance is or is not a member of a particular category." The analytic definition of uncle "suffices to enable an investigator to predict whether any new kin type he encounters (such as Fa Mo Si Hu) is or is not uncle" (122-123).

Since all of these questions are necessarily set in an emic framework, I interpret the foregoing to mean not that the investigator will be able to tell whether Fa Mo Si Hu is or is not an uncle, but rather that he will be able to tell that the indicated actor-type will be called "uncle" by any informant. If this is correct, we are justified in doubting that the rules do indeed accomplish what Frake claims they do, since all that is involved, as in the case of *bedults*, is that the rules permit us to tell when an informant will say that he will say a particular person is uncle. When it comes to actual verbal behavior, the actor-type in question may never in fact be called uncle. But this is an empirical question, involving the observation of actor-types in multi-actor scenes, and the development of indices of referential agreement.

Ethnosemantics: Ethno-Actonics

The existence of natural language terms for denoting non-verbal behavior stream entities has been a source of much confusion in the social sciences. That natural languages contain special terms and implicit systems of classification for behavior and behavior-group entities is no less expectable than that they should discriminate between trees and bushes or the moon and the sun. It is a curious epistemological failure which has led to the separation of ethno-actonics from the rest of ethnosemantics. Instead of valuing ethno-actonics for what it is—verbal behavior—anthropologists have tended to value it for what it is not—a substitute for operationalized intersubjective actonic analysis. To be sure, ethnography ought properly to be concerned with these behavior and group-denoting words and phrases, with establishing their semantic equivalencies, and with exploring their referential meaning within the local habitat. But, as will be seen, one cannot avoid actonic analysis by appealing to the population's own system for describing its vernacularly perceived actor-types, episodes, scenes, permaclones, etc. To establish the referential meaning of natural terms, some intersubjective set of criteria based on replicable operations must underlie the language in which the referential meanings are specified. An intersubjective behavior stream language must be operative if one ethnographer is to tell another what a given population means by its terms, even though, in the local habitat, the referential meaning is pragmatically unambiguous. The pragmatic sort of intersubjectivity achieved in a given population's local environment may be entirely adequate for biosocial survival, but it is invariably inadequate for scientific understanding, since the ethnographer, unlike the native actor, is confronted with all the intergrades culled from the study of other populations.

The Role of the Informant

Although the informant's description of the behavior stream is inadmissible as a substitute for the ethnographer's etic analysis, ethno-actonics does have a significance extending beyond mere verbal behavior. In practice, the ethnographer may quite reasonably use his informant's vernacular description of behavior stream entities as a starting point for his own analysis. This tactic is based upon the assumption that complex interaction nodal chains, scenes and serials, nomoclones and permaclones cannot be repeated or regrouped unless the actors themselves are guided by some conscious and pragmatically verified, roughly intersubjective plan or map of behavior.[4] Knowledge of these plans helps the ethnographer to form an approximate idea of what to expect in a given scene and where to look in order to find the population's primary nomoclonic and permaclonic types. Hence they are of immense value for previewing a population's scenic and clonic repertories, and for singling out those aspects of the population's behavior stream vital to the ethnographer's theoretical interests. The ethnographer may get a good idea of what happens in an actual fishing scene by talking to one of the fishermen. But it is a rare informant, indeed, who will describe the scene so well that the ethnographer might just as well have dispensed with an actual voyage.

I do not wish to give the impression that this problem exists only for those ethnographers striving for actonic purity. Even by vernacular standards an informant's descriptions of behavior stream events are seldom satisfactory. Like the ethnographer, he cannot possibly hope to render a completely faithful description of a fishing scene. He too must somehow pick out the highlights. But unlike the ethnographer, his selections are not governed by any systematic principles. He invariably knows much more about what happens than he is likely to tell. For example, before going out in a boat myself, I was told that it is the task of the prowman to haul up the anchor. Observation revealed that all four crewmen pulled on the rope after the prowman had taken in the slack. My informant, of course, had known this as well as he knew his own name, but it was a detail which had simply not been featured in his version of the fishing behavior plan.

Ethno-actonics thus provide a kind of rough map of the territory over which the ethnographer must travel. It would be uncharitable both to myself and to most ethnog-

[4] For discussion of cognitive plans and maps, see Wallace, 1962; Miller *et al.*, 1960; and Tolman, 1948.

raphers to propose that the recording of behavior plans is a useless activity if pursued as an end in itself. A poor map is better than no map at all. I have no misgivings, however, about rejecting outright the ill-founded notion that the ethnographer's principal task is to record the plans of behavior by working with a handful of informants and that such plans constitute the basic reality of culture.

Ideal and Actual Behavior

The concept of ideal and actual culture or behavior is popularly intended to emphasize the fact that people *sometimes* say they behave in one way while actually behaving in another. The foregoing discussion compels us to take a second look at the word *sometimes* in this formula. The implication is that people sometimes really do behave the way they say they do. But as we have just demonstrated, behavior plans are never precisely fulfilled in actual behavior, even by vernacular standards. An informant's rough map of an interaction episode chain or a permaclone never corresponds exactly to the ethnographer's version of the same events. The only exception of which I can conceive would be the case where the ethnographer had taught the informant to use an operationalized data language. In all other instances, the informant's referential meaning is based upon unstated and hence nonreplicable operations. Were it otherwise, there would be no need to develop a scientific data language.

The term "ideal" is sometimes given the additional nuance of ethically expected or desirable behavior. The informant says what people *ought* to do, but, upon inspection, they are seen to do something else. I find this concept hard to reconcile with the existence of behavior plans. If complex behavior stream events are assumed to be guided to some extent by the behavior plans of the actors, then it follows that such plans must exist for deviant or ethically undesirable behavior as well as for any other kind. A man, after all, does not lightly undertake the task of robbing a bank. The bank president has a plan which he thinks decent people ought to follow if they want to get money out of the vault; the bank robber has another plan. Ideal behavior in its moral sense, therefore, turns out to be either a simple case of a plan which is incomplete or incongruent with respect to the ethnographic data language description of the actual events, or of a plan which is elicited from only a particular actor-type, and which is not shared by others.

The disparity between two actors' cognitive maps may even extend to scenes in which they carry out complex interaction nodal chains. Surprisingly little evidence supports the prevalent notion that shared goals, common motives, or shared cognitive structures must underly complex cultural performances. Wallace and Atkins (1960) have demonstrated that theoretically the "same" interaction behavior is perfectly compatible with several different cognitive maps. Indeed, according to Wallace: "Not only *can* societies contain subsystems, the cognitive maps of which are not uniform among participants; they *do,* in fact, invariably contain such systems. . . . Many a social subsystem simply will not work if all participants share common knowledge of the system" (Wallace, 1962:39-40).

The Meta-Taxonomy of Verbal Things

The study of verbal behavior leads to an astonishing paradox. Up to a certain level of abstraction, verbal things are the most perfectly operationalized entities in the social sciences. Beyond that level, intuition, subjectivity, and guesswork reign. For dealing with such units as phones, phonemes, morphemes, and grammatical categories, linguists have constructed logico-empirical systems of great predictive and retrodictive power. But when it comes to such entities as mazeways, themes, cognitive maps, behavior plans, values, ideology, ethos, world view, national character, the operational precision characteristic of the treatment of lower-level verbal phenomena has seldom been in evidence. There are many indications, however, that this situation is rapidly changing. Extremely sophisticated operational procedures for the study of verbal cultural things are now being developed by Anthony Wallace, Floyd Lounsbury, Harold Conklin, and Ward Goodenough, to mention only a few of the anthropologists active in the field of componential analysis and transformation theory. It is hoped that an equal amount of attention will eventually be directed to models for the analysis of nonverbal behavior, a task which has been even more neglected, even though it is a logically prior one.

10

The Nature of Culture

As long as the definition of culture is conceived in terms of essences, archtypes, final causes and other miasmas rising from the intellectual swamps bequeathed to us by Aristotle and Plato, the age-old conceptual vagueness will remain. If we adopt an operational, actonic model of culture, many of the most hoary issues at once receive their well-merited quietus.

What Is Culture?

Culture is actones, episodes, nodes, nodal chains, scenes, serials, nomoclones, permaclones, paragroups, nomoclonic types, permaclonic types, permaclonic systems, and permaclonic supersystems. Culture is also phonemes, morphemes, words, semantically equivalent utterances, behavior plans, and many other emic things. Culture is any and all of the nomothetic nonverbal and verbal data language units previously defined. None of these units is more or less cultural than the others, although it is possible to classify them into a hierarchy of progressively more abstract constructions, depending on the number of logico-empirical operations which they embody.

Since cultural things are scientific concepts, and since the unique, or that which happens only once, must forever remain beyond the pale of science, I prefer to regard all idiographic instances of the nomothetic units as not-culture. They are rather the raw materials from which cultural things are constructed.

Is Culture Real or Merely an Abstraction?

Cultural things are as real as any knowable abstraction and as abstract as any knowable reality. The position that some empirical things are real while others are merely reifications of abstractions is so transparently a product of a prescientific mentality as to render further comment embarrassing.[1] To say that cultural things are abstractions or constructions, however, is not to embrace a philosophy of solipsistic idealism.

The basic premise of empirical science is that there are things outside of the observer which no amount of merely logical manipulation can create or destroy. The nature of these things can be known only by interacting with them. Since there are many ways to achieve this interaction—many optional operations—all things in their knowable state are *partially* the creations of the observer. This view is not at all antithetical to the strictest versions

[1] Cf. Radcliffe-Brown (1952:190): "We do not observe a 'culture,' since that word denotes, not any concrete reality, but an abstraction, and as it is commonly used, a vague abstraction. But direct observation does reveal to us that these human beings are connected by a complex network of social relations." Franz Boas accused Alfred Kroeber of considering culture to be "a mystic entity that exists outside the society of its individual carriers" (Boas, 1928:235). Under attack by Bidney (1944), Kroeber decided that he had been guilty of a so-called "culturistic fallacy." Motivated by the "ardor of a new attitude" he had exaggerated and transcendentalized" culture into an entity in its own right. He rejected "the hasty and unusually hazy attitude which sees culture as a special kind of entity or substance" and took the opportunity of "publically recanting" his "extravagances and over-statements" (Kroeber, 1948:407). The futility of this gesture was noted by Phillip Bagby (1953) in a seminal article to which the present analysis is greatly indebted.

of materialism. Indeed, to insist upon the importance of an actonic approach, and the separation of verbal from nonverbal behavior, is to insist that thinking, wishing, yearning, believing, and praying cannot alter the environment. This means that if there is any consistent relationship at all between etic and emic phenomena, it can only be one in which emic things are ultimately shaped by the conditions of the material world.

Can Cultural Things Be Seen or Touched?

Actones, episodes, nodes, nodal chains, etc. are classes of events. They are logico-empirical concepts. The senses cannot perceive logico-empirical concepts; they can only construct them. You cannot touch a concept.

Can Culture Be Reduced to Psychology?

Perhaps the most ferocious paper tiger in anthropology is the threat, keenly felt by certain partisans, that the study of culture may be swallowed up by, or reduced to, the study of psychological or even biological things. Alfred Kroeber was one of those most concerned to ward off reductionism. He believed that culture was an entity *sui generis* and that it required an initial neglect of the individual if it were properly to be understood. His emphasis on the "superorganic" nature of culture provided him with some strange bedfellows, among whom Leslie White has figured most prominently. White insists not only on the autonomy of the superorganic but goes so far as to propose that any explanation of cultural differences and similarities which appeals to psychological, biological, or physical principles is heretically in error. "Culture must be explained in terms of culture" (White, 1949:141).

I should like to suggest, parenthetically, that White and Kroeber did not understand what each was getting at despite their mutual veneration of the superorganic. White's interest in the superorganic goes back through Durkheim to Spencer (who coined the term) and ultimately to Marx. For all of these scholars, neglect of the individual was quite correctly a necessary condition for the creation of a science of society (read culture) which would be capable of formulating the laws of history. Kroeber, however, never shook off his Boasian training, and specifically rejected the possibility of lawful cultural change in his monumental but ill-conceived *Configurations of Cultural Growth.*[2] His interest in the superorganic stems from his involvement with writing anonymous history or history writ large. Kroeber avoided dealing with the individual not because he thought there were superorganic laws, but because he wanted to write the history of such entities as the alphabet, plow agriculture, and dress design—things in which specific historical individuals can scarcely figure since their identity is not known. These entities, he argued, had a life of their own apart from the individuals who produced them. Hence the need for a separate science to study them.

White's rejection of individual behavior is best understood through his oft-repeated dictum that a constant cannot explain a variable.[3] Cultural differences and similarities (variables) cannot be explained by the laws of psychology (the constant) which are presumed to operate equally in all hominid populations. Hence the refrain, "culture can only be explained by culture." White's error is transparent. If anthropologists cannot solve their cultural equations given only the value of the constant, this does not mean that they can and must solve them only

[2] "In reviewing the ground covered, I wish to say at the outset that I see no evidence of any true law in the phenomena dealt with; nothing cyclical, regularly repetitive, or necessary" (1944:761).

[3] "Variations of human behavior are functions of a cultural variable, not of a biological constant. Human behavior as we find it amongst the various peoples of the world is to be explained therefore in terms of their respective cultures rather than by appeal to 'human nature' or psychological tendencies" (White, 1949: 139).

with a knowledge of the variables. Cultural evolution is surely inexplicable given only a knowledge of the laws of individual hominid psychology—a fact which, as White correctly insists, is improperly digested by many psychologically-oriented social scientists. But this does not mean that cultural evolution can be successfully predicted or retrodicted without taking those laws into account.

The fears of the anti-reductionists or super-organicists are fully matched by the fancies of their opponents who are fond of such remarks as, "In the final analysis, the individual is the locus of culture because individuals can paint their fingernails and avoid their mothers-in-law, but cultures cannot."[4] Both sides misconstrue the issue. Culture is a series of abstractions developed through the logico-empirical manipulation of data collected from the study of the observed or implied behavior of specific historic individual men and women. White and Kroeber would have us believe that one can perceive cultural things without bothering to collect such data. But whatever it is that can be perceived in this fashion (pots and inscriptions—actones or place objects) we may rest assured that no one has or will "perceive" an actone or episode, let alone a permaclonic system, without first collecting data on the actual or implied behavior of specific individuals. The reductionists, on the other hand, would have us believe that individual behavior *is* culture. This is like saying that a response is an actone, an actone is an episode, an episode is a nodal chain, a nodal chain is a permaclonic system, etc. Neither side displays the slightest understanding of the fact that individual behavior is itself an abstraction, that this abstraction is the raw material for the construction of further abstractions, that there are many levels of abstraction involved, and that culture is not merely culture but actones, nodes, permaclones, etc., each of which is called into being by different kinds of

[4] For a discussion of the philosophical issues in reductionism, see Brodbeck, 1954 and 1958; Watkins, 1955.

logico-empirical operations.[5] Both sides see the problem in terms of reductionism—how to avoid it, or how to accomplish it. But nothing could be more irrelevant to the epistemological issue really at stake. To reduce or not to reduce is not the question. What we must know is how to abstract—how to proceed from the observation of unique, idiographic individual responses to the grand supra-individual heights of super-permaclonic systems and still carry on intersubjectively viable discourse.

Do Infrahuman Organisms Have Culture?

Since infrahuman organisms do not contribute responses to the human behavior stream, they obviously do not have *human* culture. Insofar as an ant, dolphin, macaque, or chimpanzee has different body parts from that of a hominid, the actones which it performs can only be regarded as analogous to those found in human populations. Nonetheless, it is entirely possible and richly rewarding to apply a similar set of logico-empirical operations to the behavior stream of infrahuman organisms. All animals from the amoeba on up can probably be shown to have repertories of actones, episodes, nodes, nodal chains, scenes and serials. All sexually-reproducing animals probably also have repertories of multi-actor scenes and serials, and hence possibly nomoclones and permaclones. The so-called social insects, all mammals, and most birds certainly do have permaclones and possibly even permaclonic systems.

Many of my colleagues will undoubtedly be shocked by the heresy of insect culture. Accustomed to a totally unoperationalized approach to the cardinal concept of

[5] White (1949: 96-7) argues that there is no more reason for calling cultural traits abstractions than there is for calling anything else an abstraction. "A wild horse is not an abstraction. Why call a domesticated horse (a culture trait) one?" Instead of concluding that *both* are abstractions, White decides that neither is. He thus avoids the central problem which is to specify the logico-empirical nature of the abstractions involved.

their discipline, most anthropologists insist that insect societies are cultureless. The operative rationale is that insect behavior is supposed to be governed by instinct whereas human behavior is learned. This view conflicts with the fact that insects are perfectly capable of learning to run mazes and of learning to solve other problems. Insect behavior is not totally under the control of instincts, nor is human behavior totally governed by learning experience. There is an instinctive and an experiential component in all animal behavior, although admittedly the lower grades of organisms acquire parts of their response repertories under the influence of highly specific drives for which there is no exact parallel among hominids. Still, the differences involved are a matter of degree and do not justify the Aristotelian either/or approach. The dogma of a sharp break between hominid and nonhominid behavior is even more difficult to maintain, the closer one comes to the hominid phylogeny. Field studies of monkeys have revealed that response repertories of geographically adjacent populations of the same varieties differ in manner of deployment for foraging, line of march, space between animals at feeding, and perhaps signal systems (cf. Imanishi, 1960; Frisch, 1959; Simonds, 1962).

The tendency to make culture a strictly human preserve has resulted in the widely accepted view that culture is symbol-mediated behavior and that only humans can make and use symbols. (Surprisingly, Leslie White, whose uncompromising evolutionism is everywhere else conspicuous, stands on this point with the special creationists.)[6] To insist that only people can symbol is, in effect, to deny the possibility of transitional hominoid types, such as those which human paleontology has already brought to light. No one has succeeded in teaching any of the extant infrahuman hominoids to master a human language sys-

[6] "Man uses symbols; no other creature does. An organism has the ability to symbol or it does not; there are no intermediate stages" (White, 1949: 25).

tem, but it is speculation to suppose that equally negative results would have been obtained with *Prometheus transvalensis* or *Zinjanthropus*. For all we know, the man-apes did possess a highly evolved language. But no matter upon which hominoid or hominid—*Australopithecus, Pithecanthropus*, or *Neanderthal*—the honor of first symbol user is bestowed, we must sooner or later grapple with the problem that the first bona fide symbol system could not have sprung full blown from the head of some primitive genius. Language, like every other part of culture, has had an evolutionary career.[7] Since no genuinely primitive language has survived to the present, we have no really firm idea of what these transitional systems were like. But it is intolerable to suppose that on one day there were signs tied to specific stage coordinates, and that on the next there appeared situation-free symbols, grammar, syntax, and a lexicon capable of describing everything of importance in the local universe.

Advocates of this "miraculous conception" theory of the origin of language are fond of citing Helen Keller's experience in learning how to symbol. Miss Keller remembers the exact moment when she learned that "everything had a name."[8] This supposedly proves that either you symbol or you don't. Aside from the fact that Miss Keller was endowed with a very late model *sapiens*' brain which would certainly have been the envy of the first symbolers, her mentor also happened to have had the benefit of a language which was at least twenty thousand years in the making. Miss Keller did not learn that everything had a name; she learned that there was a *language* in which everything had a name waiting for her to learn. Neither she nor her teacher had to invent that language from scratch. Indeed, had this been the case, probably neither one of them would have symboled well enough to pass muster as *Homo sapiens*.

7 Dell Hymes has recently stressed this point.
8 Cf. White 1949: 36-9; Cassirer, 1944: 23-41.

Can Cultural Things Exist for Only One Generation?

Anthropologists have also sought to set off human behavior from all other animal behavior by emphasizing the traditional or trans-generational nature of human learned responses. Human populations are viewed as possessing a pool of socially-conditioned responses which are passed on from or are taught by one generation to the next. The human infant is said to go through the process of enculturation, by which he comes to share in the learning pool of the population in which he is reared.

The emphasis which anthropologists have placed upon intergenerational continuity of response repertory is responsible for a great deal of confusion in the social sciences. When culture is defined in conformity with this emphasis, it attracts the merited scorn of sociologists for its evident failure to embrace some of the most interesting phenomena in modern industrial society. If culture consists only of cross-generationally duplicated responses, what is one to call those episodes, scenes, and groups which are newly arisen in the cauldron of industrial innovation? A concept which emphasizes the ageless traditions lazily yielding to the gentle pressure of change may profitably be applied to the Arunta or the Mohave—although even here the actonic reality was probably something else—but it is certainly incongruous in the twentieth century. It is for this reason that the repetition necessary for the construction of the various nomothetic units has never in the previous chapters been defined as exclusively cross-generational repetition. The actonic approach admits both long- and short-lived nomothetic entities into the hall of culture, and hence its data language is as applicable to the behavior stream in Times Square as to behavior events in the Kalahari Desert. It is also applicable to behavior events in an ant nest or a baboon troop.

Having admitted short-lived nomothetic units to cultural status, there still remains the possibility that long-lived nomothetic units are the exclusive property of human populations. It might still be shown that human culture is discontinuous with respect to the rest of the animal world if no other organisms were found to have traditions, in the sense of a pool of socially-conditioned (socially learned), trans-generationally-duplicated responses. Yet, enough is known about infrahuman social life to render any such proposition untenable. The existence of traditions among monkey populations has already been cited. And there is every reason to believe that a large portion of the trans-generationally-duplicated responses among primates is a product of social conditioning. All primate infants, in other words, probably undergo enculturation.

On the basis of recent discoveries made at the Japan Monkey Center, John Frisch (1959:595) has suggested that anthropologists need to rephrase and refine their concepts of culture:

> It seems doubtful that definitions which strongly emphasize such concepts as social heredity, socially-acquired response patterns, learned traditional behavior will be able to do justice to what Julian Huxley has called the "uniqueness of man." To the extent to which culture is equated with learned, traditional behavior, monkeys appear to have indeed much more "culture" than anthropologists have often thought.

Even among lower organisms, traces of enculturation are visible. Successive generations of tits have learned to open milk bottles, parrots have learned to kill sheep, bird calls seem frequently to depend upon exposure to parental example. As for insect societies, it may very well be that all of the trans-generationally-duplicated episodes and permaclones (of which there are many) are totally under the control of instincts. But I think that people who have made up their minds on this subject are talking through their hats. The role of learning in establishing the trans-generational regularities of infrahuman social species has never been carefully studied. And enlightenment is certainly not advanced by dogmatically enshrining a snap judgment as the key concept of social science.

To insist, as I believe we must, that human cultural things are connected by an unbroken thread with infrahuman cultural things, is merely once again to uphold the viewpoint that all complex entities have had an evolutionary career which began with a more simple state of affairs. I have no intention of minimizing the differences between formicine episodes and human episodes. Not only are the actones involved drastically different, but the repertory of even the simplest human culture probably contains a thousand times more episodes than the most highly evolved ant colonies. The number of actone objects affected by human body motion is clearly without parallel in the rest of the animal kingdom. No other species engages in so many different kinds of mono- and multi-actor scenes; no organism comes anywhere near matching the luxurious profusion of man's permaclonic types or the awful intricacy of his permaclonic systems.

These differences between human culture and the scrawny infrahuman prototypes are proper objects of scientific description and explanation. My principal objection to those who would restrict the term "culture" to the human behavior stream is that they impede our progress toward understanding the difference between human and infrahuman cultures by defining away the problem. They put the cart before the horse. They tell us that, in general, the difference is to be understood in terms of the atrophy of instincts and the development of a unique kind of communication system. I concur wholeheartedly. But the fact remains that about particular cultural things—human or nonhuman—we are woefully ignorant about the parts which instincts and symbols play. Just what proportion of the human episodic repertory is actually learned through the mediation of symbols? Just how complicated can socially-conditioned permaclones get in the absence of a fully-evolved symbol language? Precisely what is the role of instinct and learning in a particular episode or scene, human or infrahuman? Until we learn the answers to such questions, the self-appointed guardians of man's noble aloofness from the rest of the animal kingdom might very well profit from a second look at their intellectual bed-fellows.

What Is the Difference between Social and Cultural Things?

The unfortunate historical series of events which led to the academic schism between cultural anthropology and sociology has polluted social science with the unopera-tionalizable distinction between social and cultural things. In the development of the data language of groups, it was clearly demonstrated that behavior units are the source of group entities, and that groups may in turn be used to identify behavior units. Culture does not consist of a social level and a cultural level, or a social aspect and a cul-tural aspect. As noted in Chapter 5, the number of para-groups in a given population is related to the number of different episodes, while the number of nomoclonic and permaclonic types is strictly governed by the number of different kinds of multi-actor scenes. How anyone can seriously propose that the study of behavior units and social groupings should be carried on separately, let alone that we need a separate discipline for each, is beyond me.

Many anthropologists who hold that social and cultural things are distinguishable, nonetheless urge that they be considered as closely related phenomena. But to say that social and cultural things are "different aspects of the same thing" or "opposite sides of the same coin," does not tell us what we want to know—namely, how the operations for identifying group units differ from the operations for identifying behavior units. Certainly, an endogroup is dif-ferent from a multi-actor scene, and certainly everyone would agree that endogroups and multi-actor scenes are related. But the question is, can one be identified without at the same time fixing the nature of the other? S. F. Nadel insists that social facts are two-dimensional. "Like any two-dimensional entity, they can be projected on to one or the other co-ordinate, and so viewed under one or the other aspect" (1951:79). Nadel does not mean by this merely that one can tell the difference between a group (social thing) and an institution (cultural thing). He means that groupings which belong to the same taxon may be associated with patterns of behavior of widely differing types. They are independent variables!

> . . . If we go beyond one society or culture, the two "orders" appear as independent variables in a much fuller sense of the word. Here the same kind of grouping will be visible, not only in a series of different action patterns, but in different series of this kind, and the same institution will be found to mobilize different kinds of relationships and groupings. Thus the family may in one society operate in the contexts of infant care, education, religious observances, and economic production, and in another in the contexts of infant care, political activities, and legal responsibilities; similarly, the institutionalized tasks of education may in one society be entrusted to the family and kinsmen, and in another to age grade associations, secret societies, or the State. (1951:ftnt., 78–79)

We are confronted here with a lesser miracle, a kind of holy duality. Two things are the same and yet they are different; two things are different and yet they are the same. This miracle is achieved by never telling us what episodes, scenes, and serials are relevant to the definition of the family, nor what nomoclones and permaclones are relevant to the definition of education serials. Thus we may happily strip away scene after scene from *The Family,* and group after group from *Education,* and we are still left with *The Family* and we are still left with *Education.* What Nadel fails to tell us is that the commonality between family in the first instance and family in the second cannot simply reside in the fact that these are two sets of genealogically related people. Somewhere along the line these two sets must also exhibit some behavior in common. A biological father and son are not members of a nuclear family if the father is divorced and living in another city. The concept of nuclear family makes sense only if we know that fa, mo, so, and da behave in certain ways. It would almost seem as if Family for Nadel is a Platonic essence. Take away the shadow families on the wall of the cave (culture) and Family is still there burning bright in some realm of superior reality. This archtypical mode of thought preserves many social anthropologists from realizing that one might very well argue that groups with, and groups without religious scenes and productive scenes ought not to be called by the same terms. As always, the decision to withhold or bestow logico-empirical identity is an option contingent on what uses are to be made of the broader versus the narrower category.[9]

In the thinking of at least one famous anthropologist, the distinction between the social and the cultural was nourished by the putative differences between insect and human societies. According to Alfred Kroeber, since ants have society but not culture, there must be a difference between the social and the cultural (1948:9). In a very murky passage, Kroeber identified society and culture with the opposite sides of a sheet of carbon paper (1948:10). By the light of the previous discussion about the existence of insect episodes and permaclones, I interpret this metaphor to mean simply that there is a difference between a behavior unit and a group unit. Even if we deny culture to the ants on the grounds that ant episodes are instinctual, we are not entitled to conclude that ant be-

[9] Edmund Leach's search for "the essential sociological nature" of Indian castes is another example of this archtypical mode of thought among British social anthropologists. Caste can be regarded optionally as restricted to India or found elsewhere, depending on how much detail about scenes and serials is furnished. The crucial question is what kinds of theories about socio-cultural processes result when one option rather than another is taken.

havior units can be profitably operationalized without reference to group units, or that ant group units can be profitably operationalized without reference to behavior units. Even less can we conclude that in the human behavior stream, where everything is presumably learned, there exist operationally separable social and cultural levels of phenomena worthy of description.

At times, the separation of the social from the cultural is merely a matter of distinction between verbal and nonverbal behavior. Talcott Parsons, for example, equates culture with cognitive maps which lie behind or orient social action.[10] This usage is not only unnecessary, but is clearly counter to the intentions of the overwhelming majority of anthropologists. I personally do not care what term we use to designate the sum of the behavior stream entities. "Social action" is as agreeable to me as "culture." By all means let us call actones, episodes, nomoclones, permaclones, etc., "social action." But then let us get rid of the term "culture" and cease to perpetuate the delusion that the study of culture and the study of social action merit separate disciplines. This, of course, does not amount to an endorsement of Parsons' theory of social action which I consider to be a totally unoperationalizable actor-oriented, subjective approach to behavior stream events. The real issue is not whether we use the term "culture," but whether we accept the operations by which actones are built up into permaclonic systems.

For those who still seek some employment for the term "society," there remains a very well-established usage which I wholeheartedly endorse. In this usage, society denotes the population whose behavior stream is the object of study. Since there are no perfectly isolated

10 "The keynote of the conceptualization we have chosen is that cultural elements are elements of patterned order which mediate and regulate communication and other aspects of the mutuality of orientations in interaction processes. There is, we have insisted, always a normative aspect in the relation of culture to the motivational components of action; the culture provides *standards* of selective orientation and ordering" (Parsons, 1951:327).

human populations, the boundaries of a given society may fluctuate according to the nature of the observer's research interests. Hence, one may speak of the society of a primitive village or tribe, the society of a small town in the United States, the society of the town and its hinterland, the society of the whole country, Western society, or the society of all mankind. Each of these societies produces a behavior stream. Society is thus a group of people, while culture is the sum of the entities constructed from the observation of the behavior of a society's actors.

Appendix
A Nodal Count

To render explicit the rules applied in the nodal analysis of the sample episode chain (see pages 73–80), let us follow the chain for some distance:

Episode 1 has no antecedents and hence no functional requisites.

Episode 2 (pull drawer) required (1), since the drawer could not have been opened in the manner described without the actor first getting close enough to it to pull on it.

Episode 3 (pick up knife) required both (1) and (2).

Episode 4 (push drawer) required (1) and (2), but not (3). One might argue that, with the removal of the knife from the drawer, the drawer was modified, and hence the closing of the modified drawer was dependent upon removing the knife (3). The opposite conclusion would seem equally tenable: removing the knife did not modify the drawer, but merely transposed the knife which was not a part of the drawer.

It would be fruitless to seek an absolute answer to which position is the more correct, since the issue of whether the knife is or is not part of the drawer cannot be resolved by appeal to common macrophysical principles. Accordingly, I shall simply adopt the procedural rule that the mere removal or insertion of objects from or into nontransportable containers does not alter the container.

Episode 5a (carry knife) clearly required (3), (2), and (1).

Episode 5b (walk to refrigerator) required none of the antecedent links of episode (5a), since the actor was not physically obliged to walk to the cabinet and pick up the knife in order to walk to the refrigerator.

Episode 6 (pull refrigerator door) merely required walking to the refrigerator (5b).

Episode 7 (pick up potatoes) required both getting to the refrigerator (5b) and opening the door (6).

Episode 8 (push refrigerator door) required opening the door—it would not have swung shut unless it had been opened—which in turn required walking to the refrigerator.

Episode 9a (carry knife) required nothing which happened after the knife was picked up from the drawer. That the knife was carried first to the refrigerator and then to the table does not by its mere occurrence demonstrate the physical necessity of carrying the knife to the refrigerator in order to carry it to the table. Count is (3), (2), (1).

Episode 9b (walk to table) could have been accomplished without carrying anything.

Episode 9c (carry potatoes) required nothing having to do with the knife. Count is (7), (6), (5b).

Episode 10a (put down knife [on table]) poses the question as to whether the table is to figure in the nodal count as an actone object. To put the knife down, there was no need for the actor to put it down on the table. Hence, walking to the table is not a requisite antecedent. Since the opposite view might also be cogently argued, we again resolve the issue by formulating a rule: the place at which an object is put down is irrelevant to the count of requisite antecedents for the manipulation of the object. In order to put the knife down, it merely had to be picked up (3), which in turn required (2) and (1).

Episode 10b (put down potatoes [on table]) when reckoned in conformity with the above rule requires neither the walk to the table nor the carrying away from the drawer. Count is (7), (6), (5b).

Episode 11 (walk to cabinet) required none of the previous behavior.

Episode 12 (pull door open) required only (11).

Episode 13 (pick up frying pan) required (11) and (12).

Episode 14 (push door of cabinet) required (13), (12), and (11).

Episode 15a (walk to table) required none of the previous behavior.

Episode 15b (carry frying pan) required (13), (12), and (11).

Episode 16 (put down frying pan on table) in conformity with the rule formulated in (10a) does not require walking to the table. The pan could have been put down as soon as it had been picked up out of the cabinet. Count is (13), (12), (11).

Episode 17 (sit down), regarding the total body as the actone object, and applying the same rule as in (16) and (10a), required no antecedents.

Episode 18 (pick up knife). The manipulation of the actone object in this episode is the "same" as that featured in (3). To pick up the knife required only walking to the drawer and opening it.

Episode 19 (pick up potato). The actor now has the potato and knife in hand, just as was the case before she put them down on the table. Clearly, she did not have to walk to the table and put the potato down in order to have the potato and knife in her hand. Count is (7), (6), (5b).

Episode 20 (pull knife under potato skin). In order to cut the skin, the actor had to get the knife from the drawer (3), (2), (1) and get the potato from the refrigerator (7), (6), (5b). She did not have to walk to the table, sit down, or put the knife and the potato on the table.

Episode 21 (pull knife through skinless potato). In this case, the skinless potato (and the knife) is(are) the actone object(s). Hence, cutting the skin off is a requisite for slicing the skinless potato. That the slices fall into the frying pan is irrelevant at this point. However, when the frying pan itself later becomes an actone object (25), all the behavior that went into bringing the frying pan and the potato slices together will become part of the nodal count. Count is (20), (7), (6), (5b), (3), (2), (1).

Episodes (19), (20), and (21) were now repeated for other potatoes. These repetitions are not plotted on the graph.

Episode 22 (put down knife) required only (3), (2), (1).

Episode 23 (pull garbage pail). To pull the garbage pail, it was necessary to get within reach of it (15a).

Episode 24 (push peels) required that they be detached from the potatoes (20), which in turn required (7), (6), (5b), (3), (2), (1). That the peels were on the table and that they fell into the garbage can is not at this point relevant to the count.

Episode 25a (stand up) required (17).

Episode 25b (pick up frying pan). The actone object is now the frying pan with its contents. As distinguished from nontransportable containers, the addition of the potato slices to the pan is regarded as having modified the object which is being picked up. Hence, all of the episodes responsible for the procurement and processing of the potatoes, plus the episodes responsible for procuring the frying pan, are now counted. To put the slices into the frying pan, the skinless potatoes and the pan had to be brought together. Episodes (21) and (20) were part of this process; episodes (19), (18), and (17) were not, for reasons previously stated. The potato slices would not be in the frying pan, however, unless they had been put into it. This was accomplished by placing the pan under the potatoes. Hence, the placing of the pan (16) is now counted. This in turn required (15a), (15b), (13), (12), and (11). It also required the placing of the knife and potatoes accomplished in (9a), (9b), (7), (6), (5b), (3), (2), and (1).

Bibliography

Ayer, Alfred (ed.). *Logical Positivism.* New York: Free Press of Glencoe, 1959.

Bagby, P. "Culture and the Causes of Culture," *American Anthropologist*, 55:535–554, 1953.

Barker, Roger and Herbert Wright. *Midwest and Its Children.* New York: Harper and Row, 1955.

Benedict, Ruth. *Patterns of Culture.* Boston: Houghton Mifflin, 1934.

Benjamin, A. C. *Operationism.* Springfield: Charles C. Thomas, 1955.

Bertalanffy, L. von. "The Relativity of Categories," *Philosophy of Science*, 22:243–263, 1955.

Beuttner-Janusch, John. "Boas and Mason: Particularism versus Generalization," *American Anthropologist*, 59:318–324, 1957

Bidney, D. "Concept of Culture and Some Cultural Fallacies," *American Anthropologist*, 46:30–44, 1944.

———. *Theoretical Anthropology.* New York: Columbia University Press, 1953.

Birdwhistell, Ray. *Introduction to Kinesics.* Louisville: University of Louisville, 1952.

Black, Max. *Language and Philosophy*. Ithaca: Cornell University Press, 1949.

Bloch, B. and G. Trager. *Outline of Linguistic Analysis*. Baltimore: Linguistic Society of America, 1942.

Boas, Franz. *Anthropology and Modern Life*. New York: W. W. Norton, 1928.

Braithwaite, R. B. *Scientific Explanation*. Cambridge: Cambridge University Press, 1953.

Bridgman, P. W. *Reflections of a Physicist*. New York: Philosophical Library, 1955.

———. *The Logic of Modern Physics*. New York: Macmillan, 1927.

Brodbeck, M. "Methodological Individualism: Definition and Reduction," *Philosophy of Science*, 25:1–22, 1958.

———. "On the Philosophy of the Social Sciences," *Philosophy of Science*, 21:140–156, 1954.

Bruner, J. S., J. Goodnow, and G. Austin. *A Study of Thinking*. New York: John Wiley and Sons, 1956.

Cassirer, Ernst. *An Essay on Man*. New Haven: Yale University Press, 1944.

Chapple, E. and C. Arensberg. "Measuring Human Relations: An Introduction to the Study of the Interaction of Individuals," *Genetic Psychology Monographs*, 22, 1940.

Conklin, H. "The Relation of Hanunóo Culture to the Plant World," Doctoral dissertation. New Haven: Yale University, 1954.

Dettering, R. W. "Linguistic Superfluity in Science," *Philosophy of Science*, 26:347–354, 1959.

Dodd, Stuart. "Operational Definitions Operationally Defined," *American Journal of Sociology*, 48:482–489, 1942.

Donagan, A. "Explanation In History," *Mind*, 58:145–165, 1957.

Evans-Pritchard, E. E. *Social Anthropology*. Glencoe: Free Press, 1951.

Feigl, H. and M. Brodbeck. *Readings in Philosophy of Science*. New York: Appleton-Century-Crofts, 1953.

Firth, Raymond. "Contemporary British Social Anthropology," *American Anthropologist*, 53:474–489, 1951.

Fortes, M. "The Structure of Unilineal Descent Groups," *American Anthropologist*, 55:17–41, 1953.

Frake, C. "Cultural Ecology and Ethnography," *American Anthropologist*, 64:53–60, 1962.

———. "The Diagnosis of Disease Among the Subanum of Mindanao," *American Anthropologist*, 63:113–132, 1961.

Frisch, J. "Research on Primate Behavior in Japan," *American Anthropologist*, 61:584–596, 1959.

Gerard, R., C. Kluckhohn, and A. Rapoport. "Biological and Cultural Evolution," *Behavioral Science*, 1:6–34, 1956.

Goodenough, W. H. "Componential Analysis and the Study of Meaning," *Language*, 32:195–216, 1956.

Hanson, Norwood. *Patterns of Discovery*. Cambridge: Cambridge University Press, 1958.

Harris, Marvin. "The Economy Has No Surplus?" *American Anthropologist*, 61:185–199, 1959.

Harris, M. and C. Kottak. "The Structural Significance of Brazilian Racial Categories," *Sociologia*. In press.

Harris, Zellig. *Methods In Structural Linguistics*. Chicago: University of Chicago Press, 1951.

Hart, Hornell. "Operationism Analyzed Operationally," *Philosophy of Science*, 7:288–313, 1940.

Hymes, Dell. "The Ethnography of Speaking," m.s. n.d.

Imanishi, Kinji. "The Social Organization of Subhuman Primates in Their Natural Habitat," *Current Anthropology*, 1:393–407, 1960.

Kaufman, Felix. *The Methodology of the Social Sciences*. New York: Humanities Press, 1958.

Keller, F. and W. Schoenfeld. *Principles of Psychology*. New York: Appleton-Century-Crofts, 1950.

Kluckhohn, C. *Mirror for Man*. New York: McGraw-Hill, 1949.

———. "Universal Categories of Culture," in A. Kroeber (ed.), *Anthropology Today*. Chicago: University of Chicago Press, 1953.

Kroeber, A. *Anthropology*. 1948.

———. *Configurations of Cultural Growth*. Berkeley: University of California Press, 1944.

———. *The Nature of Culture*. Chicago: University of Chicago Press, 1952.

———. "White's View of Culture," *American Anthropologist*, 50:405–415, 1948 (also in Kroeber, *The Nature of Culture*).

Kroeber, A. L. and C. Kluckhohn. "Culture: A Critical Review of Concepts and Definitions." Papers of the Peabody Museum of American Archeology and Ethnology. Cambridge: Harvard University, 47:1952.

Leach, E. R. (ed.). *Aspects of Caste in South India, Ceylon and Northwest Pakistan*. Cambridge: Cambridge University Press, 1962.

Lewin, Kurt. *Field Theory in Social Science*. New York: Harper Bros., 1951.

Logan, Frank *et al. Behavior Theory and Social Science*. New Haven: Yale University Press, 1955.

Lounsbury, F. G. "A Semantic Analysis of the Pawnee Kinship Usage," *Language*, 32:158–194, 1956.

———. "The Varieties of Meaning," Institute of Languages and Linguistics, Monog. No. 8, Washington: Georgetown University, 1955.

Lundberg, G. A. "Operational Definitions in the Social Sciences," *American Journal of Sociology*, 47:727–743, 1942.

Mandelbaum, M. "Societal Facts," *British Journal of Sociology*, 6:305–317, 1955.

———. "Societal Laws," *British Journal for the Philosophy of Science*, 8:211–224, 1957.

McGee, C. D. "Who Means What By 'Synonymy,'" *Inquiry*, 2, No. 3, 1959.

McKinney, J. P. "Knowledge and Experience: Comment on a Paper by L. von Bertalanffy on 'The Relativity of Categories,'" *Philosophy of Science*, 24:349–356, 1957.

Miller, G., E. Gallanter, and K. Pribram. *Plans and the Structure of Behavior*. New York: Holt, Rinehart, and Winston, 1960.

Morris, Charles. *Signs, Language and Behavior*. Englewood Cliffs: Prentice-Hall, 1946.

Murdock, G. and C. Ford. *Outline of Cultural Materials*. New Haven: Human Relations Area File, 1950.

Nadel, S. F. *The Foundations of Social Anthropology*. New York: The Free Press of Glencoe, 1951.

Nagel, Ernst. *The Structure of Science*. New York: Harcourt, Brace and World, 1961.

———. "Teleological Explanation and Teleological System," in Feigl and Brodbeck, *Readings In Philosophy of Science*, pp. 537–558, 1953.

Osgood, C. E. *The Measurement of Meaning*. Urbana: University of Illinois Press, 1957.

Pap, Arthur. *Semantics and Necessary Truth*. New Haven: Yale University Press, 1958.

Parsons, Talcott. *The Social System*. Glencoe: The Free Press, 1951.

Pike, Kenneth. *Language in Relation to a Unified Theory of the Structure of Human Behavior*, Vols. 1–3. Glendale: Summer Institute of Linguistics, 1954–60.

Pittenger, R., C. Hockett, and J. Danehy. *The First Five Minutes*. Ithaca: Paul Martineau, 1960.

Quine, W. V. *Word and Object*. New York: John Wiley and Sons, 1960.

Radcliffe-Brown, A. R. *Structure and Function In Primitive Society*. London: Oxford University Press, 1952.

Rapaport, Anatol. "Mathematical Biophysics, Cybernetics, and Significs," *Synthese*, 3:182–193, 1957.

Sapir, E. "Do We Need a Super Organic?" *American Anthropologist*, 19:441–447, 1917.

———. *Selected Writings of Edward Sapir in Language Culture and Personality*, David Mandelbaum (ed.). Berkeley: University of California Press, 1949.

Simonds, Paul. "The Japan Monkey Center," *Current Anthropology*, 3:303–305, 1962.

Simpson, G. G. *Principles of Animal Taxonomy*. New York: Columbia University Press, 1961.

Skinner, B. F. *The Behavior of Organisms*. New York: Appleton-Century-Crofts, 1938.

———. "Operational Analysis of Psychological Terms," in Feigl and Brodbeck, pp. 585–594, 1953.

———. *Science and Human Behavior*. New York: Macmillan, 1953.

Spence, Kenneth. "The Empirical Basis and Theoretical Structure of Psychology," *Philosophy of Science*, 24:97–108, 1957.

Stein, M. *Explorations in Community*. Doctoral dissertation. New York: Columbia University, 1959.

Suttles, W. "Affinal Ties, Substinence, and Prestige Among the Coast Salish." *American Anthropologist*, 62:296–305, 1960.

Tolman, E. D. "Cognitive Maps in Rats and Men," *Psychological Review*, 53:189–208, 1948.

Vayda, Andrew. "A Re-examination of Northwest Coast Economic Systems," *Transactions of the New York Academy of Sciences*, 23:618–624, 1961.

Vidich, A. and J. Bensman. *Small Town in Mass Society*. Princeton: Princeton University Press, 1958.

Wallace, A. F. C. and J. Atkins. "The Meaning of Kinship Terms," *American Anthropologist*, 62:58–81, 1960.

Wallace, A. F. C. "Culture and Cognition," *Science*, 135:351–357, 1962.

———. *Culture and Personality*. New York: Random House, 1962.

Watkins, J. W. N. "Historical Explanations in the Social Sciences." *British Journal for the Philosophy of Science*, 8:104–117, 1957.

———. "Methodological Individualism: A Reply," *Philosophy of Science*, 22:58–62, 1955.

Wax, Murray. "The Limitations of Boas' Anthropology," *American Anthropologist*, 58:63–74, 1956.

White, Leslie. *The Science of Culture.* New York: Farrar, Straus and Cudahy, 1949.

Whorf, B. *Language, Thought and Reality.* New York: John Wiley and Sons, 1956.

———. *Selected Writings of Benjamin Lee Whorf.* John B. Carrol (ed.). Cambridge: Technology Press, 1956.

Withers, R. F. J. "Epistemology and Scientific Strategy," *British Journal for the Philosophy of Science,* 10:89–102, 1959.

Ziff, Paul. *Semantic Analysis.* Ithaca: Cornell University Press, 1960.

Index